At 29, within a month,
I left my husband, lost my job, went broke, and had almost all of my belongings stolen. Yet somehow the only question that kept going through my mind was . . .

who the hell am I?

This memoir recalls my stumblings through my 30's as I tried to figure it all out. From finding my biological parents and discovering where I came from, to exploring my sexuality and finding out who I wanted to become.

I tried to be brutally honest, so prepare yourself to cry, laugh, cringe and maybe judge, sometimes all in one paragraph.

Hopefully, at the end you'll see that not only can you survive, but you can thrive . . .

especially in a great pair of red heels!

A Memoir

Lost: Woman Found: Child

by M. Page Jones

Let There Be Light
PUBLISHING, LLC

www.ltblpublishing.com

LET THERE BE LIGHT PUBLISHING
Copyright 2012 by Let There Be Light Publishing
All rights reserved, including the right to reproduce this book or portions thereof in any form whatsoever.
For information contact publisher@ltblpublishing.com

ISBN-13: 978-0615700243 (Custom)
ISBN-10: 0615700241

Author's Note: This memoir is drawn from memories of real events that took place in my life. Names have been changed to protect the privacy of those people. Memories are often fickle and over time and with retelling sometimes details change. I have drawn from personal journals, family and friends to make this memoir as true to the original facts as possible.

Printed in America.
Published simultaneously in Europe.

Found: Woman / Lost: Child
A Memoir

DEDICATIONS:

To Amy for Paris.
To Alicia for the jar of buttons.
To Preston for the healing.
To the little girl for the journey.

A Memoir

Lost: Woman
Found: Child

PROLOGUE

My childhood consisted of children's homes, to foster homes, to an adopted family with ultra-fundamentalist Bible beliefs, to a half dozen Christian schools all while living in the middle of Ohio Amish country.

My teens were full of Bible camps, to church 4 times a week, to practicing piano 3 to 4 hours a day, to Christian schools that averaged about 30 students, K-12 and who didn't allow dating at all.

In my 20's, I went to the Christian college both my parents worked at, I worked two jobs, started to date in college (where touching was not allowed, and all dates took place in front of chaperones with carried wooden rulers to make sure that you were exactly 12" apart), to getting married with a mutual virgin.

Then at 29, I suddenly discovered I had no idea who I was.

I had been told my whole life how to think, dress, feel, and believe. I decided after much heart-wrenching, soul-searching days and nights to leave my husband and figure out on my own who the hell is this woman I see when I look in the mirror.

This book is not a chronological account of my life. Rather it is about how in my 30's, I discovered who I was, who I wanted to be and also who I didn't want to become. Lessons usually people learn throughout their whole lives that make them who they are.

I wish I could tell you that I stood on the edge of my newly made freedom and jumped with a smile into the undiscovered abyss.

I think it was more like I sort of tripped, fell off the edge and watched as my white- knuckled hands slowing slipped off, and I fell backwards screaming.

So, here is what I learned, sort of like the "lessons", during that free fall. This book is about people who came into my life showing me the good and the bad but always pointing me in the direction of finding "me".

ONE

Person: My Biological Mother

Lesson: Love is not always a given.

Lesson: Sometimes the dog wins.

Animal shelters have always been a very hard place for me. It's not only the sadness of it all, and the wanting to adopt every single furry face, it's deeper then that. Having been placed in a children's home at a very young age, I always felt a sort of kinship with the animals. People give you shelter and food but that's about all. There are no hugs and kisses and cuddling. They are there to do their job and go home. Once in a while a soul will invest in you but you know better then to get attached. On adoption days, people would walk by and study you, maybe pat you on the head, but then walk on by to the next hopeful.

I was at the local humane society with my then husband, Patrick, to adopt a kitten. Patrick had already moved onto the "kitten room" but I had stopped outside a glass door that looked into four rows of frenzied dogs locked inside steel mesh crates. A few stopped barking to study me as if seeing a fellow adoptee that knew their pain.

To understand a lot about me, we have to go back to when I was almost two years of age. . . a truly defining moment in my life.

I was living as most children do with my mother and father and my dog, Blackie, who was indeed black. My father had just been diagnosed with a heart strain and was told to rest up in a wheelchair which he interpreted as: take the $26,000 of settlement money that he had won when he strained his heart at work, gamble it all, gamble more than he had, get his ass kicked for not having the money, allowing him a valid excuse to drink because he lost the money, and wish my mom, a fellow alcoholic, well on her way to work.

Well over 27 years later and after having spoken to my dad on the phone (more about that later) about the whore mother who up and left us, I decided to get her side of the story. With the help of a newly found aunt, I dialed the number.

A man answered the phone. My aunt had instructed me to tell her husband first who I was as often my mother was drugged up or drunk or suicidal.

"Hello, my name is Page Jones. I think that your wife, uh, Shirley is my mother."

Silence.

"Who is this?"

"I think that Shirley is my mother. My dad is David Paulette? I was born in 19—"

His sudden roar startled me so much even my cat who was sitting on my lap jumped.

"Shirley! Get in here. There's some girl on the phone that says she's your daughter with that fucking Paulette guy."

The phone became muffled and I could hear more yelling. After awhile, a woman's voice spoke.

"Hello?"

I felt a thousand words and sounds fill my mouth at once hearing my own mother's voice. People take knowing the sound of their mother's voice so for granted. I let that single word wash over me.

"Hello?" she said again.

My rehearsed script stood me in good stead.

"Hello, my name is Page Jones. I think that you might be my mother? I was born in 1969 to a David and Shirley—"

"Oh, no."

Through the years of wondering whom my real parents were, the daydream had transitioned throughout my life. As a small girl, I had studied each face and each car that came near me to see if they recognized that I was indeed the princess who had been stolen away from a grieving king and queen. As I grew, it changed to parents who were so poor and homeless but loved me so much that they sobbed as people ripped me out of their arms for my own good. As I matured, I imagined all kinds of scenarios and the gush of warmth that would fill their voices as I uttered the words to them, "I think I'm your long lost daughter."

The melodious, life-fulfilling consonants and vowels of "oh, no" were never what I had dreamt of.

"Maybe I'm wrong. Maybe I have the wrong person," I stuttered.

"No, I'm your mother." She said it like someone was calling to see if she was registered to vote. "How did you find me?"

I explained the years of searching with the stubbornness that I must have gotten from one of them. I found my father and he in turn helped me find her. Silence.

I couldn't hold it in anymore.

"Why did you leave us? I mean, I was 2 years old."

She paused. The silence seemed to go on for hours. I wondered if she really hadn't thought this day might come and prepared something? Or did the reality of me just disappear like she did?

"You don't understand. He was always drinking and doing stupid stuff. I couldn't take it anymore. He—he was always talking shit and running out of money. I just didn't know what to do!"

Now the silence was coming from me. Did she just say that?

"So you just looked at me then my dog and made a decision?" I really hoped my sarcasm would register but not so much that she'd hang up.

Maybe she had actually grabbed her purse, her keys, stopped and looked at my drunk father slumped over in his wheelchair, looked at me playing on the floor by his feet, switched her attention to the cute black poodle, and . . .

"I just made a decision."

She took the dog, left and never came back.

Yes, you read that right. She took the dog and left her two year old daughter with the drunk.

"So, why did the dog win?" I wanted to ask. Instead I asked, "Why did you leave me behind?"

She sighed heavily. "I couldn't live with your father anymore. We weren't married. I mean he tells everyone we were but we weren't. And if I took you-he was obsessed with you-he'd never leave me alone. I just needed a clean start."

She needed to start over . . . apparently with the dog.

For years I thought while this was a horrible thing to do as a mother, it really didn't determine who I was as a person.

I was wrong. Standing in that animal shelter, I suddenly pictured my dog in one cage and me in the next while my mother walked up to each and studied us. Which one would suit her new life? Which one would be less trouble? Which one was housebroken?

Had I somehow known as that chubby white-blonde child that at the moment she was making this decision? Had I studied her face with large, soft eyes begging her to take me with her? Would she have? Or had the dog just been that much cuter with maybe a head tilt to the side that had won her over? I pictured her enthusiastically pointing to the poodle and saying "definitely that one." Maybe when she walked out of our house through the front door, she had paused, reached in and scratched behind my ears, promising "someone will adopt you soon."

Five foster homes and a children's home later, she was right but I had sat in what felt like a shelter kennel too long by then.

As we wrapped up our first conversation via phone, she felt compelled to make sure that she was not indeed a bad person.

"I knew your dad would fuck up and they'd take you, you know, the State. And then you'd get a good home where he couldn't find you. I mean when they called me and told me that I needed to sign over my rights -I—I did feel bad and a couple days after signing it, I called and asked the judge if I'd done the right thing. I'd moved on, I had a new life. It really was all for the best, see. I mean, it all worked out . . . right?"

I didn't know how to answer that.

"You did have a good life, right? I mean, that's why I did what I did."

"And what if I didn't have a good life? What if you're rolling the dice with a 50/50 chance that went the wrong way?"

Again there was silence.

"But-but it did. Right?"

Suddenly, I just felt very, very tired. I wanted to yell and scream at her saying horrible things. I wanted her to say — what was the magical word or phrase I was waiting for to take all the pain and abandonment away? Some charmed verbiage that would heal it all.

Having talked to her for just a few minutes, I knew she would never have said it anyway. It just wasn't in her.

She ended the conversation by telling me if I ever came to Ohio she would talk to me. Currently living in North Carolina, I wasn't sure when I would be able to get to Ohio. (Of course, I had no clue I would be there visiting my father within the week in a race against the Grim Reaper.)

Here is where the story has a true complete circular pattern. A week later, a card arrived from my mother. As I hurriedly opened it up, I began to read words of sorrow and sadness and a plea to never contact her again as I had almost ruined her life.

"I have a son. He doesn't know about you and it would kill me for him to find out. He's just graduating high school. Please! Just stay away.

Go on and be happy. Forget about me. Know I care about you but I can't risk having you in my life and my son finding out what I have done. Goodbye."

I stared down at the handwriting with its shaky strokes and odd slanted lines and thought, "she did it again." Walked out. And to add to it all, I had a brother. A child that she loved, protected, defended. Another child she was capable of loving so much that she didn't want him to know about me, her "mistake." So, it wasn't that she was incapable of being maternal, it was - well, logically, it had to be me who just wasn't lovable. Right?

After reading and re-reading, I decided to employ one of my emotional survival techniques that had stood me in good standing throughout my life, I thought of the bright side of it . . . at least this time she chose another human being over me. That was a step up.

As I went into the kitchen and poured myself some water, I willed myself not to feel it. Not to fall apart. I would not pick up the nearest object and hurl it against the wall. I would breathe. Deep calming breaths. I wouldn't let her have the power of hurting me yet again. I slapped the tears out of my eyes, and pushed back my shoulders.

But then as I closed the card to put it on the counter, I saw the picture on the front cover. A cute puppy with his head tilted sideways looking at the camera with warm, puppy eyes. I flipped it over and saw that it had been a FREE card from the Animal Humane Society.

I then employed my second survival tactic . . . laughter. Ironic laughter that makes you laugh and cry at the same time.

Sometimes I wonder to this day if she ever thought about the endless abyss of irony in her choice of that card. If she ever thought of any of her choices.

A couple of weeks later, a large envelope arrived. Evidently, my mother had told her sister about the call and she sent me pages and pages of photos. Faces of cousins, aunts, uncles, grandparents, my half-brother, all strange faces that somehow looked familiar because so many looked like me. Also, there was a complete written out on lined notebook paper the complete history of my family. Birth dates, death dates, marriages all filled the pages.

I quickly flipped through the photos and continued to be

amazed that face after face looked like me. Unless you've been adopted or never met your father or mother, there is no way to describe this. I've literally sat at my computer for over an hour now trying to say the right things to make you feel it.

I know this isn't quite it but it must be like when a blind person who has never seen their face is able to see again. They get to see their relatives' faces and see how much they look alike. You find yourself doing that stupid thing they do in Lifetime movies where you trace their faces with your fingertip and cry. You suddenly feel that your feet aren't always just standing on the ground but roots are now growing that are securing you into a more complete idea of who you are.

I wiped the tears from my eyes, turned the page and there she was. No mistaking her. I was the spitting image of her. Pale, wearing glasses, reddish-blonde hair. Same nose, lips, jaw line. It was like looking at a twin.

I did not run my fingertips over her photo. I just stared at it for hours. From now on when I pictured my mother taking the dog and leaving, the woman had a face. She had hands and legs. She had eyes and a mouth. She was real. Too real.

For the first time in my whole life, I could stop wondering who she was or what she looked like. I could just look in the mirror. It was both a blessing and a curse. Does that make sense? I'm trying to make sense of it all myself even to this day.

TWO

Persons: Patrick & Grandpa

Lesson: Sometimes people really do love you.

Lesson: If you stare long enough, you can catch
Mrs. Butterworth moving.

    I couldn't believe him when he said it. Early on during our courtship the inevitable topic of family had come up between my future husband and I. Understandably, I declined going first with my tragic "sir, may I have some more" life story, so he graciously agreed to start.
    "I don't remember one bad day growing up with my family," he repeated again to my still-frozen-in-amazement expression.
    "Not one day. Not one day of. . . I don't know, like being yelled at or hit or made fun of? Not one?"
    "Nope."
    Now you may be asking yourself why a boy with a sweet face,

a pure soul, and a wonderful family life would even notice me with my haunted expression and tendency to flinch when touched. It was like a beautiful swan swimming by stopping to fall in love with one of those birds that look like a pigeon and a duck got drunk one night.

For the next eight years, he would be the one who made this amazing nest of softness for me to heal. Layered with support, humor, and patience, this place was warm and comforting and allowed all the nightmares and demons of my past to be sorted through.

He endured the first four months of our marriage with me very sick with the effects of endometriosis, along with my tendency of waking up screaming from nightmares. I think it was particularly harsh when in the middle of the night his arm or leg would brush mine and I would in half-sleep sit bolt upright in our bed staring with no recognition at him. He would gently say my name and urge me to lie back down.

I guess this might make a little more sense if you knew that I had had no one in my bed with me until our wedding night. We were both virgins. Well, I assume you can still claim virginity when you were deflowered as a child. I've always been slightly confused about that.

On our wedding night, I remember being in bed with a white satin gown on (to point out even more my purity, I guess). The room was cold. It hurt when he slowly put himself inside of me but I didn't make a noise because I didn't want to ruin it for him.

With my beautiful off-white, garden-length wedding dress hanging on the door beside the bed, I made my mind go somewhere else until it was over. It wasn't that I didn't love him or desire him, but with the endometriosis and the rape as a child, it wasn't exactly a happy place for me. Our marriage was more of an amazing friendship than a passionate one. It was warm, it was full of light, it was soft, it was . . . new to me.

Shortly after I was adopted at the age of three by these strange new people who insisted I act like their daughter, my adopted mom began trying to "drive the demons" out of me, so to speak . . . actually no, she really said that that was her mission from God.

She began to spank me after the social worker had made her final assessment that I was in a good, loving home. My first memories are of being tossed into a wall and held down on the floor while being hit with a wood paddle. These sessions were then followed by a forced apology on my part, and an impassioned prayer for my soul on hers.

I feel it necessary here to put in that my adopted father was a very loving man who always treated me like his own flesh and blood. However, he had no real say in the household as the very powerful "properly submissive" wife was in charge.

She did make a point of beating me mostly when he was not home. In my teens, she even made sure my brother wasn't there so no one could back my story. This was a way of life for many of my friends. We were all raised independent Bible which meant we were taught to believe everyone who didn't believe exactly like we did were going straight to hell. Also, God hated women who wore eye makeup, pants and had short haircuts. All gays were contagious and God hated them most. Oh, and drinking of any kind was wrong and so was divorce. Although apparently you could be forgiven of your divorce and remarried but only if the church voted and agreed. The poor woman or man would have to stand in front of the church and plead their case, followed by a group prayer and a vote. Homosexuality was not given a chance. You were just Sodom and Gomorrah walking around spreading AIDS with your fingertips.

My closest friends were four daughters of our preacher, all with appropriate biblical names. Often their mother would assess that they had sinned and drag one of them into a back bedroom and begin to hit them. The rest of us would stand where we were and shuffle our feet back and forth and play with the buttons on our appropriate-length jumpers. We would wait for them to come back out so we could go play. It was the oddest version of "leave no man behind" that was ever created.

For years, three of the four girls would pull all of their eyelashes and eyebrows out in stress. I began a sort of OCD around the age of 12 where every time I walked through the kitchen I would have to touch the burners in a clockwise direction even if the burner was obviously bright red. I burned my fingers on the stove probably over a dozen times. I didn't know how to stop and I thought I was going crazy. After the fifth time, I laid on my bed with bright, red blisters on my fingertips, crying. My mother walked in with fresh laundry and looked down at me, snorted and rolled her eyes.

"Don't think I'm taking you to the doctor. You did it to yourself. So stupid." As she walked back out, she looked over her shoulder with some parting wisdom. "You need to go pray about it."

That is how a fundamentalist cures OCD. No therapy. No "let's talk about it." No medication. No seeing it as a cry for help. That is how all of our odd behavior was handled in our pious community.

Even odder is if you came down with a serious ailment, then God was trying to teach you something. If it was just the sniffles, then you must have forgotten to have your devotions that day. I remember thinking when I was little that God seemed to have alot of time on His hands.

Last I heard of my best friend, the oldest one, Sarah, was pregnant with her eighth child in nine years of marriage. Her husband believed that birth control was abortion.

"He says if God wants you to have a baby, it happens. Who are we to judge God's wisdom?" She told me over the phone, crying and now pregnant for the ninth time.

"My doctor told me if I come back pregnant again, I – I – I need to ask you something, do you think it's a sin to take birth control without telling my husband? I'm — —I'm just so tired."

I wanted to jump in my car, drive to Ohio and grab his Bible off the nightstand by their marital bed and beat him with it followed by handing him back his penis after ripping it off.

"Listen. Your husband is an idiot. Birth control prevents the egg and sperm even meeting and shaking hands. It's not abortion and if that jackass would like to be pregnant for over nine years and push nine kids out of his asshole, then he can have a say. Damn, Sarah."

So, in our small town of a hundred people, there was enough neurosis in the name of "not sparing the rod" to go around. Of course, once we moved to South Carolina, it didn't stop even though I was a senior in high school. The day of my 18th birthday (I had been held back in preschool a year due to my lack of social skills. Yes, I flunked preschool.) I had apparently done one of my mortal sins, looking at her the wrong way on the way out of the kitchen.

"What was that look?" she snarled. I paused, freezing my expression to see if my eyes were in mid-roll or my lips were in the end stages of a smirk.

"What?"

"I am so tired of your bad attitude. When is it ever going to stop?" She pointed to the nearest room, my brother's bedroom, and insisted that I wait for her there.

I heard her going from room to room, mumbling and looking for something to punish me with. I calmly waited on the bed picking at the little balls of material that covered the old worn out red, white, and blue bedspread. I heard utensils rattling in kitchen drawers. Closet doors being slammed open and shut. For a brief moment, I was glad that Dad's glock was locked away since she seemed particularly pissed off.

She arrived back slightly out of breath and produced a wood yardstick.

I remember looking at it and thinking "are you kidding?"

"Lay down on the bed on your stomach."

Knowing if I didn't obey right away, it would only get worse from there, I laid down.

She soon learned that it was hard to control 36 inches of flimsy wood. So she ended up hitting me pretty much all over…back, thighs, calves.

Arriving late to school, I rushed to open up my locker and get my books together since I was now late from the corporal punishment. "Happy birthday, Page!" My best friend, Casey, yelled as she grabbed me in a tight hug. I shuddered from the pain. She pulled back and looked at my face as my eyes filled with pain and tears.

Suddenly, all my friends appeared with balloons and flowers and circled my locker. Casey grabbed all of us and pushed us into the girl's bathroom. Without asking, she pulled up the back of my blouse. Welts were beginning to form and looked particularly horrible against my very pale skin. I remember thinking that I didn't want to be late for class as I had never gotten a demerit before and took some pride in that.

I heard the first sniffle behind me. Then another. I turned

around and saw them all standing behind me, still holding onto those silly balloons and flowers. Thankfully, I didn't need to tell them what had happened. After a year of knowing me, they knew the answer. They all stood around me being careful not to touch me and cried.

I did not.

I had learned to make it not hurt inside. I had learned to put the pain away and put on a smile for those around me because I didn't want them to feel bad. And when it got particularly horrid, like when I refused to cry which resulted in her hitting me until I did, I would go to my room and remember the man who made me feel safe and loved . . . my adopted grandfather.

At the age of three, between the new found hate of being hit and all the past wrongs of my biological parents, various foster homes, and the sexual attack, at the age of almost four, I was in survival mode. Ever watchful. Ever scanning rooms and spaces before I entered them. Reading people's eyes and energy to see if they were friend or foe. Like a hitman who never sat with his back to a door, I was always alert.

So after a few weeks in my new home, my family took me to a type of baby shower-welcome-to-the-family dinner at my new grandparents' house (my adopted dad's father). I put on my survival blank stare and sullen expression and got into the car.

My mother insisted that my stick straight hair be curled and tugged and pulled to bend into this vision she had in her head. Apparently, she was a Shirley Temple fan. She demanded I hold her hand as we walked up the sidewalk, something I hated as I didn't allow anyone to touch me. It actually seemed to hurt my skin. Hugs and pats on the backs caused me to wince.

"You know, Page, it wouldn't kill you to smile." She told me through gritted teeth. At that moment if it had, I would have been okay with it.

As we walked into the living room, there sat around 25 or 30 of my new aunts and uncles and cousins, first and second generations, all sitting in a semi-circle around the room.

I felt my adopted father gently push me forward.

"This is our little girl, Page," he said.

I remember a lot of teeth. Lots of them being flashed at me. Forced smiles. Nice smiles. "Let's get this over" smiles. A couple a little crazy looking. More then a few with missing teeth.

Then towards the left-hand side of the group in a simple wooden chair sat a man with silver hair, dark rimmed glasses, suspenders holding up gray pants, and a checkered shirt. He had a smile on his lips but that isn't what I saw first . . . his eyes smiled. They twinkled like contagious mirth was dying to burst out of them. Like a belly-full of laughter was waiting to pour out and you knew you would join in and feel its lightness wash over you like warm water.

As people around the room were still being introduced to me, I firmly disentangled my fingers from my adopted mother's and strode with purpose towards the man. I felt the room sort of fade away the closer I got to him. Without thought, as if being pulled in by some unseen tether, I crawled onto his lap, and wrapped my thin arms around him. With a deep sigh, I buried my face in his neck.

He smelled of tobacco and hard work. His energy seemed. . . light and soothing. Like nothing I had sensed before.

He seemed to instinctively know not to pull me in tight but to just let me sit there. All he did was lean down and in the softest, West-Virginia mountain accent say, "Page, I'm your grandpa."

Up until a few weeks before he passed from lung cancer, he

repeated that story often. Proud that I knew he was safe. Proud that on that day, I never left his side and refused to let anyone else touch me. Proud that he became my friend, my safe place.

I don't know how I knew he was safe. How he would become my best friend. Through the years we would spend hours together sitting on the front porch. He would have his pipe full of cherry tobacco in one hand and a fly swatter in the other tapping out with his feet some mountain song he heard in his head. Always with a small mason jar full of ice tea that he would wave with at cars as they drove by the one main street in our small town of less then 100 people.

He would tell me story after story about growing up in West Virginia. His tales were magical and always well-timed in their delivery. He was a master with his words. He talked about working in the coalmines, about the day he saw my grandma for the first time. Of horses he had ridden in the mountains, and the moonshine he had made. He laughed at the jokes he had pulled like the time he tied firecrackers to a cat's tail and tossed it into a hollow log.

One of my biggest regrets is not sitting down with a tape recorder and taping him as he mesmerized us all. Occasionally, Grandma, with her short 5' 1" frame and barrel-shaped body sporting a floral housecoat, would walk in and correct a detail here or there, but the stories always pretty much stayed the same. He was such a master that you never grew tired of them.

Those twinkling eyes were also full of mischief. He loved to play practical jokes on his grandkids and we ate it up. When I was around six years old, for almost a year he had me convinced that the bottle of Mrs. Buttersworth that always sat in the center of the kitchen table next to the vinegar and sugar bowl moved when I wasn't looking. She also talked to him but only when I left the room. He started this over pancakes one morning.

"Page! You missed it again! She just moved! Actually, she just winked at me. Well, I'll be—!"

I shifted my weight forward in the chair and stared at her.

"No," he insisted, "You need to look out of the corner of your eye. She won't do it if you stare directly at her. She's a little shy."

I turned my head towards the rooster-fabric curtained kitchen door. Carefully, I moved my eyes to the left and waited.

My grandmother who we all called "Grams" walked in carrying her knitting needles and some yarn. She stopped and put one chubby arm on her ample hip.

"James, what are you doing to the child?"

"Shhhh....she's trying to catch Mrs. Butterworth move. She just keeps missing it!"

Grams slapped him on his shoulder. "James, stop that nonsense before her eyes stick that way." He tugged on his suspenders and laughed a warm laugh.

In his cleverness, he waited until Grams walked away and then leaned in to whisper. "She doesn't like Mrs. Buttersworth because she's constantly flirting with me, but you should keep on trying to catch her. She'll move for you too."

He treated all twelve of us grandkids that way and the fact that he didn't exclude me and actually seemed to enjoy doing it to me more made me feel like family. All the generations of his family treated me like their own. Never once did I feel adopted. The old generation and the newest generation of them embraced me like I had never felt before. I began to trust again and when it became unbearable at my house with my mother, I would flee to that home and feel safe.

That's what Patrick was. He was like another version of my

grandfather. He was an amazing friend and husband.

So, when it came time to walk away and discover who I was, it was sort of like walking away from my grandfather. A man who was good, with great character, funny, full of life, full of hope, and had done nothing but love me.

The last year of our marriage, it had been building for awhile. This itch to discover more, well, of everything. I had wanted desperately for Patrick and I to go to New York or LA or somewhere where we could pursue our film careers. I had pushed him to make his film, pushed him to write his scripts, pushed him to not be complacent with his career. Meanwhile, I had been pushing myself to be curious about everything around me. Like when a baby bird begins to look down and contemplate flight.

I began to understand that I had some natural abilities with film production and when I started to be flown around the country to produce independent films, I started to see that the world was bigger than our single-wide trailer in North Carolina. I wanted more. I wanted to learn more about me, about others. And I wanted to do it with him. He did not.

"You're okay if I just pack up and go to New York City for a year. Just pack and go."

He shrugged. "Yeah, if that's what you need to do for yourself. Go. I'll be here and wait for you."

I stared into his eyes wanting to see . . . I didn't know what. Suddenly, my soft resting place was beginning to turn into a bed of concrete. I felt betrayed. Even this man would not fight for me. Not fight to stand shoulder to shoulder with me. I think in his heart, he thought that it was being generous of him to allow me to go explore. He didn't understand I wanted to do it with him.

I began to resent him. We lived together, we worked together, we played together, we did everything together. And now, he didn't want to do this together.

I thought a lot about it. Maybe I should just go. I pictured myself in a city that can swallow you whole.

Then it hit me. I was about to return myself. Just like all those foster families had done. That version of me that was the scared little girl who jumped at her own shadow and rarely looked people in the eye. Who trusted very few and disliked everything she was too afraid to try. I was returning her. I didn't want to be her anymore, even in the slightest.

One morning in our eighth year of marriage, I woke up on the couch where I had begun to sleep for over a month. Patrick walked into the kitchen to make some coffee and I proceeded to rip his heart out.

"I can't do this anymore."

"What?"

"Us."

He sat down in his favorite recliner and stared at his feet. His ears began to turn red.

"Do you want to try counseling or something?"

"I don't think it would help."

The redness now crept down his face. I could see the veins in his neck start to pulse and his hands were gripped together tightly. These by the way are the first signs of a dying heart.

"So you don't love me anymore?"

"Babe, I will always love you. You saved me. You made me better. You made me feel I can be strong. I just can't live with you anymore. We've become . . .good friends and that's not enough for me anymore."

I didn't hear him begin to cry. I just saw one large tear splash onto his foot. I stared at it as it slowly slid onto the dark blue carpet.

I needed him to understand.

"I don't know who I am. I need to know who I am. I've spent my whole life doing what everyone told me to do. For god's sake, my mom controlled every aspect of my life. Even my hairstyle, makeup, clothes…god, even my underwear choices until I left home at 24. The Christian schools and colleges told me what to think and feel and do. I went to being a wife and never once stopped to think 'who the hell am I?' I don't know what I like or dislike. I am afraid of too many things. And I know as long as I have you there to protect me, I'll never figure things out for myself. I have no clue who I am. I've tried my whole life to be good enough for people. So, they won't return me like . . . like a pair of shoes that don't fit or something. Pleasing everyone and never once stopping to…."

I stopped. I just stopped and cried. We sat in silence in opposite corners of our living room. Our cats, Laverne and Shirley, wandered in and sat down between us, staring, like they knew something was about to happen.

Then suddenly he got up, still looking at the floor. He walked over and grabbed his car keys. As he opened the front door, he turned.

"I'm going to go see a movie. You've got three hours to pack your things and leave." Then he walked out.

I began to pack with one hand and with the other I picked up the phone and cried for almost the full three hours with my best friend and film editor, Alice. I paced our kitchen with the cats turning their heads to watch my frantic path yelling over and over "what have I done?" I felt enormous guilt and hypocrisy.

I sobbed into the phone, "I mean, could I act more like my biological mother? My current life doesn't suit me anymore so I up and just leave? What kind of monster am I? Am I just like her? Damn, what if I'm just like her, that horror of a mother?"

At least, unlike my biological mother, I didn't take the pets with me, I thought as I drove away in my jeep with two suitcases in the backseat. Not sure why I found comfort in that.

I had promised Patrick until death do us part eight years ago. And if I had been the same person or even slightly the same person now as the girl who said those words, I would have drawn my last breath beside him. But she was gone.

A few days ago almost seven years later, I heard from Patrick. He said that he was moving to LA to pursue his career. That large regret I had carried around with me through those years began to heal. He was doing it. On his own. Doing exactly what I wanted for him all those years ago. What I had wanted for us both. Here I was still in North Carolina running a graphic design company and he was leaving the nest in full flight.

I told him "I am so proud of you, and if you forget to mention my name in your Oscar speech I'll kill you."

He laughed. "I promise."

And then he packed up his belongings and began to journey down the large fork in the path of his life. I feel honored to have walked with him for awhile. A man of such great character.

To this day, I have not found a more honorable man. Patrick and Grandpa Page were giants in my life. They were my safe place. They were my "home."

THREE

Person: My Biological Father

Lesson: Finding your biological father is sometimes not how you dreamt it would be.

Lesson: Feeling like you're caught in a Jerry Springer show is not a good feeling.

I know I don't talk much about my adopted mother's side of the family. I didn't get to see them as much as my dad's side. After all, in my town of 100 people, I was related to about forty of them and a dozen or so more residents treated us as family. Everyone knew everyone. Everyone knew everyone's business. You knew who drove what and who did what for a living. In fact, I was rarely called by my name and was almost solely referred to as "Johnny-Madison's-little-girl."

This Norman Rockwell-esque town was very safe. As kids, we would wander around the streets on our bikes until the streetlights kicked on. We'd go and knock on neighbors' doors and come in for Kool-aid and cookies. It makes me sad that kids have to live in such fear today.

The two elderly sisters who lived a block down and two houses up, the Burn Sisters, would reward my brother and I for showing up on their porch with a ten gallon bucket strapped to my neck and two wooden stakes to play drums with while my brother would blow on a large conch shell that he had found in a yard sale for a nickel.

We would belt out hymns and they would clap and open their door to us. One sister would put out the cookies and milk while the other would go into the living room and play the organ singing show tunes that I had never heard before. Growing up and until the age we left home, we were allowed to listen to hymns and classical music only, although occasionally Mom would slip on a vinyl record of Streisand or Karen Carpenter. I loved that.

There were very few kids in our town of 100 people. Most of them lived on the edge of town in a trailer park. We weren't allowed to play with them unless they came to our church (which consisted of three or four families) or our Vacation Bible School. So I mostly grew up in the grown up world.

We did have a lot of cousins that we got to see at my grandparent's house when we would have family dinners. They didn't go to church at all so we weren't allowed to play with them outside of family reunions or if we were all digging potatoes in my grandpa's potato patch.

During these family reunions, all five of my dad's brothers and sisters would come and bring their spouses and all their kids. Often it would be up to thirty people there. Even great uncles and aunts would show up. My Great Uncle Cecil would take out his teeth and chase you with them. My Great Uncle Orville was completely blind by the time I met him. I'll never forget the first time we met, he walked up to me and ran his fingertips over my face.

"My, but aren't you the prettiest little girl I've ever met!"

Grandma would cook for days for these events and put all us grandkids to work in the garden or churning butter (she insisted on making her own) or helping clean out the garage so everyone could sit outside in the shade.

While everyone was setting things out for the dinner, Grandpa would sit in his lawn chair in the driveway with his fly swatter and tell his tales and occasionally swat one of us kids on the backside as we ran by. It took me a long time when I was first adopted to comprehend sitting at a table with a family and eating a meal let alone having dozens of people around you asking you questions about school and friends and making sure I stayed out of the sun since I would burn in about thirty minutes as they all soon learned.

They would have their fights. Grandpa would become peacemaker. Grandma would shove food in front of the aggrieved parties and insist they break bread together. Neither one of them got too involved in their children's lives as far as passing judgment.

The only real drama that Grandpa inserted himself into was when my Aunt Emma was about six months pregnant with her sixth child. Neither Aunt Emma or Uncle Tom worked but they drew a good amount of welfare and government food.

One day her second oldest ran the mile and a half to Grandpa and Grams house. He burst into the kitchen.

"Daddy's done beat momma bad. She's bleeding down her legs. She needs to go to the hospital!"

We all knew he beat her and the kids. It was known but not

talked about. Somehow that kind of stuff was frowned upon but apparently not something Jesus or his followers got involved in.

They got her to the hospital and soon learned that she lost the baby.

On hearing the news, I guess Grandpa had had enough. He quietly got up, set down his wooden pipe still burning the strong cherry tobacco inside, went into the closet we weren't allowed to go into as kids. He pulled out his favorite rifle. He went back to where his pipe was, picked it up and finished smoking it as he carefully cleaned then loaded the weapon.

He went outside to the garage, climbed on top of his riding lawn mower and drove to his daughter's house. Neighbors and locals saw him riding with the rifle resting on his hip and they all knew what it was about.

He parked and went into the first single-wide trailer perched on cement blocks. Having no success at finding the offender, he carefully opened the back door and walked over the large piece of plywood that was held up on either side by stairs into the next single-wide (my relatives version of a doublewide) and found him passed out in a chair.

The story goes that Grandpa calmly walked over to the chair, put the rifle to his son-in-law's chest tapping him with the end of it. The half drunk man woke up to see the business end of the firearm pointed right at his chest. With those warm hazel eyes turning into a cold shade of steel Grandpa softly said, "You lay another finger on my daughter and I will pull this trigger. Do you believe me, son?"

The drunk man stared back at my grandfather, and knew he was telling the truth. He tried to bluster out an explanation but all Grandpa did as a response was cock the rifle. Silence followed.

The family I had been adopted into was complicated and full

of characters. They loved each other fiercely. Grandpa was very well loved but could also be feared. Not because he was violent, but because you feared letting him down or him being disappointed in you. I've seen a grandkid do something bad and Grandpa just look at them, shake his head and look away. It never failed to make the offender instantly cry no matter the age . . . it just killed you.

That's what I always thought of as a good father. Someone you wanted to please because they made you feel loved and had expectations of greatness for you. Someone that you knew even if you messed up, you would never doubt their love for you. I have to say that my adopted dad was alot like that to me. If he ever used the word "disappointed", I would burst into tears and feel so awful. Of course, on the other hand, his wife could yell and hit me all day and I just felt pissed off. I did however, learn the unique gift of being able to cry on cue. That came from her insisting on hitting me with a belt or a board until I did. This skill would have come in handy if I'd ever decided to become an actress.

I often wondered what my life would have been like if my biological father or mother had been allowed to keep me. Years before finding them, I spent a lot of time on and off searching. I wanted to know my roots. I had tried several times to get my adopted mom or dad to tell me but they always told me that the judge and social worker had told them nothing.

Actually, when I was in high school and still trying to get answers, my adopted dad let slip that his wife had insisted on being the only one to know my birth name and she wouldn't tell him either. She went for years denying any knowledge.

As my 20th birthday was nearing, I started with my usual questions.

"Page! I don't know. I-I don't remember."

"You don't know or you don't remember? So you do know something!" I shouted back.

"I don't know. It started with a P. Prowley or Pauley or something."

I felt a sudden surge of hope, excitement and rage all at the same time. I think you know where the rage goes towards.

I appealed to the State Statistics Office in Ohio for a copy of my original birth certificate. They refused claiming they were sealed records. I could petition a judge for medical reasons to open the files but all I would get was a medical history. I wrote to the appropriate judge but never heard back.

I knew I had been adopted out of a home in Marion, Ohio, so I called them.

They directed me to the appropriate person who promptly told me to file with the Ohio Bureau of Statistics.

"I did. They never answered."

"Well, perhaps if you went down there in person."

"I live in North Carolina."

"Honey, we have people calling in all the time wanting their records. I tell them what I'm telling you. All you can do is write a letter and send it here. If your mother or father writes a letter and sends it to us as well, then we can make sure you all connect."

"So you're saying that I don't have the right to know my own family's medical history?"

She hesitated. "It's just not something we usually do."

Trying to keep the anger out of my voice, I took a deep breath.

"I'm sorry, what's your name?"

"I'm Miss Mason."

"Hi, Miss Mason it is nice to meet you. I'm Page. I know you probably hear this a lot but I just need you to know some things."

I claimed severe health issues and that I needed to know the medical history. I cried and begged the woman on the other end. I poured it on that I wanted to have a baby (which I didn't) and I needed to know who I was so she would know where she came from. And what if there were bad genetics in my family history? What if I brought a sick baby into this world?I laid it on thick like a Lifetime movie special of the week...premiere world broadcast version.

I could hear her hesitate again. It was going to be a lost cause.

"Page, there is only one thing I can do for you. I can fax over just the medical history sheet from your records but that's all. And all of the names will be blacked out. So, that's all I can do."

I thanked her profusely. Told her I would take what I could get. An hour later, she called to tell me that it was being faxed now.

Then she said, "Pay careful attention to the bottom of page 3. Something you'll want to be aware of. Good luck, Page."

I was puzzled until the fax came through and there at the bottom nestled in-between listings of dates of my foster homes was the one word I wanted to see "Martha."

Immediately, I wrote the local newspaper where I was born and asked them to send me the birth announcements for October 13. It took a week and I thought I was going to lose my mind.

Then, it arrived. I tore open the envelope and quickly pulled out the black and white photocopy. I quickly scanned the page. Okay, births. Now, the date. Next, scanning the list of births. There were two girls born on that day. The photocopy was blurry but I could easily make out the word "Martha" and after that "Pauley." My adopted mom had been right.

I immediately went online and found a directory of all the Pauley's in and around that area. I found thirteen of them. I sat down and wrote a letter explaining who I was and why I was writing. Over the next week, three of the letters were answered by lovely strangers who said they were not my father but who wished me well.

I decided to give it more time. Wait for the rest of the letters. As the month ended and no new returns, I felt a familiar self doubt resurface. Maybe it wasn't meant for me to know. Maybe it wasn't the right time. Maybe they wouldn't want to be found. Maybe I'd end up destroying their lives or even my own with finding each other. Maybe I wasn't ready after all. I talked myself back out of it.

Around when I was 27 and my disease was making me very ill, I decided to look up online phone listings for Pauley in Marion, Ohio. I hated talking on the phone, it made my shyness well up and sometimes I would stutter.

I stared at the phone for over an hour, silently yelling in my head to just pick up the damn phone already!

As it started to get dark in the room, I called the first one.

It rang. A woman answered the phone.

"Hi, I know this is going to sound weird, and - and I apologize for bothering you but I was wondering if you ever or any members of your family ever gave a baby up for adoption in 1973?"

"Oh, no. No, not me or any of my family. Wow, this must be so hard for you!"

"Yes, ma'am. It is. I'm sorry I bothered you."

"No bother at all. Good luck!"

The next, same thing. The third one number, again no luck. I decided to dial one more number before giving up for the day. I dialed the number.

"Hello?" A quiet, man's voice answered.

"Hi, I know this is going to sound weird, and I apologize for bothering you but I was wondering if you ever or any members of your family ever gave a baby up for adoption in 1973?"

The line was quiet and then in a slurred voice, he spoke.

"Yeah."

"What?" I shouted into the phone. "A girl born in 1969 named Martha?" The words were flying out with no possibility of a stutter.

"Yep, I'm your father."

I can't begin to tell you what that feels like. I guess the closest thing is if you thought someone you knew from a long time ago who had died called you on the phone and spoke to you. It is that stunning and jarring and unbelievable.

I asked him to repeat what he said and he said it again.

"I'm your father." Then he added very matter of fact, " I knew you'd find me one day."

It was about 4 p.m., but I could tell from his inability to complete sentences and his rambling on certain stories that he was very drunk.

"Those bastards took you away from me cuz I was sick. That no good mother of yours ran off with a man and just left you. I knew you'd come back. I lived on the same street that you was born on my whole life cuz I knew you'd be back. You'd know where to find me. They took you away but every day I went looking for you. Every day."

His sister, my Aunt Betty later would validate this fact by saying his whole life he use to wander grocery stores, the mall, department stores, parks, random parking lots looking at every blonde-haired girl to see if it was me.

He continued his tirade about my horrid excuse of a mother. I tried to ask him questions about her but everything was her fault and I was better off without her.

He began to fade and I sensed he was about to pass out. I gave him my mailing address so he could write to me and promised to call him again. Two days later, a dozen red roses showed up at my door from him.

The next day after that, his caretaker called and informed me that he had had a stroke, and it didn't look good. If I wanted to see him, I had to do it now.

Within the hour, in the middle of winter, Patrick and I (we were still married at the time - thank god he was there!), packed our bags and drove all night to get to Ohio.

The caretaker had given me my father's sister's number who had agreed to meet us that morning at Bob Evans restaurant right off the interstate, and take us to my father.

It was weird because my father told me during our first conversation that he had no brothers or sisters. No family. I found out through his caretaker that he actually had fourteen brothers and sisters with plenty of cousins. Apparently my father is bad at math.

As I walked in the door wondering which older lady was my aunt (since Bob Evans tends to draw the senior citizen), I saw an older woman with gray curly hair and a round frame look at me and gasp. She walked with a sure stride and immediately threw her arms around me.

"Marty, I can't believe it's you!"

She pulled back to study my face. Tears streamed down her cheeks. I joined her in crying.

"I knew it was you. You stand and walk just like my mother did at your age. You were named after her - Martha! And you look like all your cousins!"

We sat down and she told me everything she could think of. But she grew very sad when she talked about me being given away.

"Every year on your birthday I go to see my preacher and we pray for you and I ask God's forgiveness for being so weak."

I asked her what she meant by that. Apparently, my mother and father were both alcoholics and manic depressive. From the time I was born until the day the State took over care of me, they would show up at her doorstep, broke, with no where to live. She would take them in even though she had a husband and two sons.

She was not the only one they did this to, there was an aunt in North Carolina, a cousin in Virginia, that would open their doors to them.

Aunt Betty said we would all arrive and I would be filthy, malnourished and starving. My mom would sit for hours holding me rocking back and forth in a rocking chair not hearing my cries of hunger. (Which I know why to this day I can't stand when someone has the "jimmy" legs and is making the bed or a chair or a movie row move.) She begged them to leave me with her but sometime in the middle of the night on a random day, they would just vanish with me.

She began to do paperwork with the State to have me removed and placed into her custody. Unfortunately, tragedy struck that same month.

"My husband, my son, and my stepson were killed in a car accident. I - I just fell apart. I couldn't . . .do anything. And then, I let you down. I just terribly let you down. You poor precious baby."

All these years she carried immense guilt in not being able to be strong enough to carry on and be there for me. She sat at the table now full of empty plates and coffee cups and grasped my hands and begged my forgiveness. We cried together. The waitress brought over new napkins and patted us both on the shoulder.

"Martha - I'm sorry, is it okay if I call you that?"

"Of course."

"Thank you. Did you have a good life? A good family that you went to? It would kill me to know that it was not good."

Knowing I would be unable to be completely honest with her without ripping open the wound that had scarred over on her heart, I chose to lie.

I told her truthfully that my adopted dad had been good to me. I lied and told her my adopted mom had been wonderful as well, and that my life had been good and easy. She started to smile and glow with the release of her guilt.

"I knew if I prayed hard enough for you that it would all work out." She looked down at the cluttered table and became engrossed in neatly folding the now dirty napkin. She made it as far as two corners meeting before a sob escaped her. I jumped up from the opposite side of the table, knelt on my knees and held her.

A little later, we headed to the convalescent home where my father now called home. As the double doors slide open into the entryway, apparently word had gotten out about what was about to happen.

The hallways were lined with patients, visitors and the nursing staff. All smiled at me with joy at getting to share in this grand occasion. Several awkwardly patted me on the back and shoulders.

I don't quite understand how they thought I would want to share this most private moment with a crowd. I think too many of them watched Jerry Springer or Oprah or something and thought I needed a studio audience.

As I passed the crowd and started to walk down the final hallway full of strange smells and strong cleansers, my feet turned on their own and started running in the opposite direction. I heard "oh, nos and awwwws" as I ran.

I made it back to the foyer before losing it. I cried and sobbed like I had rarely allowed myself to do before. Aunt Betty kept calling me poor child. Patrick held me and insisted I didn't have to stay.

No, I needed to do this.

The only way I can explain it is it feels like you're walking forward but the entire inside of your body has turned around and is trying to force your skin to go the other way. Everything inside of me pushed me to not walk down that hallway, past the well-wishers and into that room. But I have always faced my fears.

Okay, one time at Universal Studios I took the chicken-out line at the new Aliens attraction. The people behind me had just seen it and were raving about it being in the pitch black and you are strapped down in a chair and they have a stereo system built into the headrest that make you feel the alien is right there complete with little puffs of air that make you think they are breathing on you. Uh……no thank you. But other than that, I have a pretty good facing-down-your-fear record.

I stood in the lobby with the double automatic doors opening and closing in accord with my now weaving to one side and the other struggling to make a decision. Finally the blasts of cold air pulled me out of my panic attack.

"I have to-have to do this."

Patrick now used to my panic attacks laid one comforting hand on my shoulder while politely holding off Aunt Betty's clumsy attempts at hugging me. He shook his head at her and she pulled back and began to rub her hands together rapidly like a neurotic grasshopper.

Patrick leaned close and whispered to me, "We can go right now. Right now. You don't have to do anything. You don't owe him anything."

I stopped and thought about what that would mean. We could drive home for another 11 hours, and I could hate myself the whole way home and most probably the rest of my life. Or I could stand up for myself for once in my life and take control. Take control. . . control. Me?

Yes, me.

I stood upright, wiped my nose with a tissue Aunt Betty dug out of her purse that smelled vaguely of mints, and started back down the hall.

People still lined the hallway, most of them were crying and some were hugging each other while wearing large "thatta girl!" smiles on their faces.

I walked into the room and Patrick wisely blocked my only available escape route with his body. And there lay my father. The man I had thought about my whole life. Every holiday. Every birthday. Every time late at night when I couldn't sleep.

I wish I could say that I looked like him. That we had the same features or hair color or eyes. I can't.

If you have ever seen pictures of people in the concentration camps during the Nazi regime, that is exactly what he looked like. Not sort of, or kind of, or if you saw him from a distance maybe…. exactly. He could not have weighed more than 90 pounds. His head was shaved, and up and down his one exposed leg were bed sores. His shrunken-in face made his eye sockets look too large for his head. Like a skeleton with the skin still on. Years of a pint of vodka a day, pain pills and never eating anything but junk food had created what sat propped up in bed before me.

He turned his head towards me and smiled, motioning with a toothpick thin arm to come in.

I had given myself permission on the drive here, and again in the hallway, that I would not temper any feelings I had when I saw him for the first time. If I felt rage, I would speak it. If I felt happy, I would show it. But what I felt was unexpected. . . pity.

How hard would you have to live a life that at the age of 54 you look like you've been buried for 10 years, dug back up, cleaned you up and propped in a bed so a long lost daughter could view your still moving remains.

We stared at each other for what seemed hours before I slowly walked over to the bed. A bruised hand with an IV attached reached with long yellow nails towards me. I flinched away.

"You are so beautiful. I knew you would be. You were such a pretty baby. You look like a young version of my mother."
Aunt Betty fussed with the sheets and covered up his leg. "I know, brother, doesn't she? I told her the same exact thing!"
I smiled a slight version of a smile.

"Hi," I shook his hand. "I'm Martha. I guess I'm your daughter."
I had wondered when I touched him for the first time if his hands would feel somehow familiar. I know it was stupid. There wasn't going to be some spark of magic that happened when our hands touched.

"Of course you are. You're my Martha. You look exactly how I remember you. I'd pick you out of any crowd. Tried to for years after they took you away from me. Never could find you though. They told me you were taken to a farm somewhere in Ohio. That true?"

I shook my head no. He huffed like he knew all along that had been a lie.

Almost without thinking about it first, I began to rapidly run through the list of questions I had made in my head on the long drive up here. I don't know why I chose the first question I asked.

"So, you and my mother were married?"

He somehow managed to pull himself up in complete rage. The sleeve of his hospital gown slide down to reveal his caved in chest and bony shoulder.

"She'd like to tell everyone we weren't married but we was. She left us. Just up and left us and took up like some whore with another man. She always was a whore."

Aunt Betty began to cluck her tongue and tell him to stop talking such ugliness. I could hear out in the hallway the crowd begin to whisper over this new piece of drama. Patrick reached out and took my hand. I could feel his warmth and support behind me.

"That whore broke her vows and took up with another man. She just left us like garbage. Took the dog though." He began to cough and a nurse appeared and helped him spit up some dark, yellow phlegm into a small metal pan. Aunt Betty moved beside me on the right and whispered that no one in the family ever believed they had been married. It was a delusion of his he felt was necessary so that I didn't feel like I had been a bastard child. Back in those days, being a bastard child was considered some kind of curse.

Throughout the next hour, with each coughing spell, my father would start a story but Aunt Betty would finish it for him.

He began to tell me about the day they took me away from him.

"They just showed up and told me you were going with them. No warning or nothing. They just took you. And you cried, cried like no little girl should ever have to. Cried more about them taking you from me then you cried when your whore mother left us."

He began to cough and Aunt Betty told me that I had been so malnourished that the bartender who worked at the bar on Main Street where my father and I lived in a room upstairs had called social services.

My father continued.

"I was sick. I couldn't work but I got me a job on a railroad. Those bastards told me I could have my own kid back if for a year I had a job and sent money to take care of you. But I got sick again. Some flu bug. I lost my job. I showed up when I was better and they said I had to sign to give you up. I told them all to go to hell." Coughing.

Aunt Betty agreed with the gist of his story but felt it necessary to fill in how he had started drinking again, and yes, he had been sick and yes, he had been sending me money and presents but couldn't hold a job to save his life. Never had been able to. Somehow being the baby of fifteen kids had spoiled him. On the evening of his 16th birthday, his brothers had taken him to a local bar, and he had never stopped drinking since that night.

I felt like I was in the middle of a bizarre tennis match in the middle of a sandstorm and the ball was my bruised heart. With each volley I could feel my insides growing tighter into their pre-existing knots.

Sensing this (probably due to the fact that my grip on Patrick's hand had become like a death grip) Patrick decided I needed a break and thought maybe we could all go somewhere where we could all sit. Aunt Betty suggested the cafeteria. We could get coffee. My father shook his head no and said he didn't need to go anywhere. A flash of stubbornness passed his face and I felt a little shock at recognizing how my face made that same expression. Patrick called it the "quiet before the silent storm – look." With this look, I began to feel that the macabre creature in front of me might very well be my father. Aunt Betty chided him for not wanting me to feel comfortable but he waved her away.

But then their stories began to agree and mingle.

They spoke of the day he had to go to court and sign the papers to give me away. Early that morning, he had shown up at her house wearing a mix-matched suit, carrying a cardboard box of my baby things. He roughly shoved the box towards her and insisted she burn it because he couldn't get himself to do it. Instead, she had placed it in her attic and for a few years afterwards, on my birthday before going to see the preacher, she would go through the box and cry.

They both went to the courthouse and my father yelled at the judge, the clerk and the bailiff for taking me away. Called them thieves, bastards, evil people.

He signed the papers, threw them at the clerk and walked out onto the steps of the courthouse where he promptly fell over with a heart attack.

"My heart broke. Them taking you away from me."

Softly beside me I heard Aunt Betty sigh and repeat. "It just broke."

I stared at him as he curled his hands into tiny, paper-thin fists and set his jaw in rage. My aunt reached and took his hand in hers. Her warm chubby fingers engulfed his and soon the rage stopped.

"I never moved. Never moved off that street. I knew if you ever came looking, you'd come to that street. Main Street. And I'd be there. And I'd go every day to the stores or the mall or just walking down the street looking for you. A little girl with white-blonde hair and chubby cheeks and freckles. I did. . . for years. Never stopped."

I knew exactly what he meant, because I too had done that my entire life. Do I look like them? Or maybe that woman? Or that family? And every wrong number that ever called wherever I was living, I wondered if it was my mom or dad searching for me but too afraid to talk to me.

I tried to think of the words to tell him so. To bond over this common trait. Then just like that, he decided he needed a smoke. He called to the nurse to get him into his chair so he could go to the smoking room.

I don't know to this day why that so deeply wounded me. He couldn't get out of bed to have a cup of coffee with us. He couldn't be bothered to be wheeled into a room where we could all sit and chat. He couldn't be bothered when I was a baby to stop drinking and get a job. He couldn't be bothered in the year he had to clean up his act and get me back to manage to do that. But here he was managing to find the desire to get up and smoke.

As I watched them lift him out of bed and place him in the wheelchair something swelled in me. He was not going to control this situation. No, I controlled this meeting. I would end it how I needed it to end.

As they began to wheel him away, I stopped the chair, put one hand on each side of the armrests and leaned in staring him directly in the eyes.

There are several kinds of rage. Rage that makes you do things without thinking. Rage that makes you literally see the color red. Rage that starts out slow and builds. Rage that starts out fast and peters out. And then there's a rage that unless you've ever felt it you can't understand it. It's a rage that makes you want to hurt someone, body and soul. Rage that wants them to crawl inside your skin and feel all your pain. Feel it wrapping around their throat and heart like a vine that would choke them with the fear, and the longing, and the desperation that fills the darkest part of your soul. Feel the small tears and deep gashes of your stolen childhood, and your constant fear that for the rest of your life you will never be good enough to have someone love you enough to never, ever, ever walk away. The kind of rage that makes you say things you thought you could never put into words.

"You hurt me. All of this . . . hurts me. That you couldn't get yourself together enough for your own child. And then you sit there and act . . .injured. Betrayed. Broken. No. you don't get the luxury of feeling that way. I do. I do. I was betrayed. I was broken. I was lost. Lost! You lost me because you couldn't be man enough to be a father."

I shook the chair in my anger. The room around me went silent. The hallway filled now only with the loud noise of the clock that hung outside his doorway. No one moved. No one breathed.

I looked down at his slight body and saw it begin to shake. The loud tick, tick, tick of the clock began to slow my breathing. And suddenly, I felt shame.

Yes, he had failed me but he had spent his entire life punishing himself for it. His heart had broken and attacked him the day he gave me up but he had had to carry it inside his chest for a lifetime. And no words I could say would make his life suddenly have meaning or worth because he never believed it did or could

I didn't want it to end like this. I leaned into him and whispered so that no one but him could hear me.

" Get better. Fight to get better. Show me I'm worth fighting for now that I'm back in your life. If you fight and start eating and doing what the doctors tell you, I'll come back in a month and we'll spend time together. I'll tell you about my life. Who I am, what I want. And you'll tell me about what I was like as a baby and what games you use to play with me and stories you use to tell me. Just do it . . do it for me."

He hung his head, and sat there for a long moment. Then he leaned forward towards me, his head barely resting on my shoulder. Instinctively, I put my arms around him and kissed his neck. Large droplets began to fall onto his hospital gown.

"Baby girl, you take care of yourself. I'm done. I just wanted to see you one more time before I died. I was just waiting."

I jerked back and shook the chair. Rage filled me again.

"You owe me to fight. You owe me that. Fight! Fight!"

He shook his head and stared at the floor. I felt numb. What else could I do? What else could I say?

Then with the softest of voices, he spoke.

"Before they took you away, I gave you a present. Do you remember?"

I had only one prize possession with me other then the shoes when I arrived at my adopted house. I never remembered why it had been important to me, and for years had kept it safe in my hope chest. I figured it meant something pretty special but had no memory of why. Now, I knew.

"It was a small pink stuffed kitten with green eyes."

His shoulders began to shake with quiet sobs. I began to cry. Everyone in the room cried. Everyone in the hallway cried.

I knew in that moment, I had given him the only thing he really needed from me. He didn't need forgiveness or love or hope because he had no need of those things. What he needed, and what I gave him was . . . peace.

I leaned into him one last time and whispered in his ear.

"I hope you've made your peace with God. Because if there is a heaven, you better be there looking out for me. Making sure I'm okay. And when I'm done here, I'm going to come find you there."

I squeezed his neck, kissed him on the cheek, and walked out of the room. I vaguely remembering people clapping as I went towards the main exit. I made it to the car before I felt my body convulse into loud sobs that soon turned into wails. I couldn't stop crying. It just wouldn't stop.

Aunt Betty told me later that for the next few days, he told all the nurses about his wonderful, beautiful daughter, and showed the picture I had left him of me. He was so happy that he got to see me one more time. So proud that I came all that way just to see him.

And now, he declared, he could die.

And three days later, he did just that.

The next week, Aunt Betty sent me a box. I opened it to see photos, paper clippings, cards, and a smaller box inside. I opened the photos first anxious to see if they were my baby pictures that I had so longed to see.

No. They were not. I don't know if any of you have family from the North but they have this odd practice of taking photos of dead relatives in their coffins. Dozens and dozens of photos from every conceivable angle were there showing his gaunt face and shrunken body.

I quickly tossed them onto the counter and moved on. There were a few condolences cards from other relatives I had not yet met. Copies of the obituary where Aunt Betty had made sure that my name was included as a surviving child. Then I opened the smaller box. Inside was what I wanted my whole life. I actually fell to the floor.

People take for granted their baby pictures. Some are even embarrassed by them. To adopted children, the likelihood of every seeing yours is miniscule but is something you long for so very much.

I pulled out a large 8 x 10 black and white photo and saw a beautiful baby girl staring solemnly into the camera as if she knew her life was already too hard. I couldn't seem to connect that that sweet baby was me. I felt sorry for her, wanted to protect her. Wanted to tell her that in the end, it would all be okay.

I studied it for along time wondering how a mother could look into that innocent face and simply walk away.

I reached back into the box and pulled out . . . my baby book! The kind of book where parents list all the important firsts. I slowly opened it to find where my mother had with great care entered all the important data of my measurements, my baby gifts, when I said my first word, my favorite toy. Filled every page up through my first birthday and then it stopped. All the other pages were hauntingly blank.

Also in the box, was the bracelet I had worn on the day I was born in the hospital. Even a few photos of me and my father as he held me in the sunlight with my almost white hair wisping in the breeze. A photo of my mother and father sitting on the couch. His face was glowing and hers looked haunted.

I kept rubbing the pages, even caught myself smelling the paper. This was something besides me that she had touched. Touched and seemed to care about attempting to be a mother. This was the only thing I had that proved she ever cared.

I've since put all the photos, clippings, and all the scraps of paper I used to find my parents into a binder. Sometimes, I'll pull it out and think about how my life began. I use it to push me forward into finding the life that little girl so rightly deserved.

FOUR

Person: Bryant

Lesson: You cannot save someone from themselves.

Lesson: Boys with long hair are often bad for you.

When I left my home I took the suitcases, my guitar, some vintage leather coats and my journals. Some friends from work let me stay on their couch along with their four cats. After the first night, I woke up and went outside to find my jeep had been broken into and all my belongings were gone. Fortunately, I had taken in my journals and one suitcase of clothes the night before. Then two days after that, I was laid off my job. My new life was not going so well. Maybe I had made a colossal mistake.

It had been awkward anyway at work as Patrick and I had employment at the same place. In between working on independent films, we had found a place that read student exit exams that worked on a project-by-project basis. We enjoyed the work and for the area we lived in, it was good pay.

We decided to be grown up about it and handle it as best we could. Thankfully, he worked the day shift and I worked the night, so our hours only overlapped by a few.

As we were walking back to the front office in the restored train depot full of brick walls and old railroad tie plank walkways, a decidedly non-historic looking character appeared. His long shaggy hair and slim black pants paired with a black tee made him look like a rocker who was about to do a photo shoot for his new album cover. Long, slender, artistic fingers held a cigarette.

Suddenly out of nowhere a cat appeared under the stairs I was walking up with Patrick and hissed. I yelped. The rocker gave a slow, lazy laugh as he flicked ashes from his cigarette.

"Cat scare you?"

I felt everything go into slow motion. Like it was a movie and someone had picked up the remote control and slowed it down. I had never talked to anyone like him and I felt my face getting red. Blushing? Really? Could I seem more of a rock-and-roll-virgin?

Patrick laughed with him and bent down to pet the stray cat. Like an idiot, I continued to stare at the man. Somehow some words I don't really remember came out and as we walked away from him, I felt my body move forward but my entire insides turn towards him. I began to feel warm and flush. I didn't know what to do with my body. So in typical fashion I tripped. I heard a soft laugh behind me.

I thought about nothing else but him the whole night as I worked. What it would be like to kiss him, hear him play his guitar (I mean, he HAD to play guitar!) For the next two days, we would wave at each other as he came out of his office that was four doors down.

Then one day as I walked into work, my supervisor stopped me.

"Some guy with long hair was in here looking for you."

I whirled around. "Long hair? For me?"

"Yeah, he said he'd stop by later."

A few hours later after sundown, he appeared at my desk with a smile that made my heart stop. I saw his eyes for the first time as apparently the vampire in him was able to take off the sunglasses after the sun went to bed.

He was beautiful. His skin was pale like mine, his hair silky and perfectly cut. His lips full and perfectly shaped.

"What are you doing after work?"

I hadn't been asked out in over nine years so I was unsure if this was a date request or just a common question people liked to ask.

"I have no plans."

"You wanna go downtown with me after?"

I nodded because the level of excitement that rose in my throat prevented me from actually making words.

"What's your number?" He handed his phone to me and I silently screamed at my shaking fingers to "stop it!" while I punched in my number. He took the phone back, slapped it shut, and walked out.

I guess technically that night was our first date. I was still wearing my little red and black sundress and red shoes when I met him later. I mean what do you wear when you go out with a guy like this? I was still into my sweet Christian girl look.

As we walked downtown from the office building, we looked like either I was taking this sinner to church with me or he was taking a sweet innocent soul straight into sin.

Now you have to understand that up to this point, I had had maybe two glasses of wine my whole life, never smoked, never did a drug stronger than allergy medicine and had slept with exactly one man. Bars and clubs were foreign to me and I felt like everyone who saw me walk into one stopped and pointed at the Christian girl from Amish country like I was a species of mold that had just been discovered on an alien planet.

So when he walked me into this downtown club, I failed to notice what it was. He shook hands with the door guy who refused to take our money to get us in saying Bryant was too much like family. The man gave me an odd look which for the next few months I would grow to get use to. The cocktail waitress hugged Bryant as well and again gave me the look.

As we followed her into the main room, I could hear people cheering and clapping enthusiastically. We rounded the corner and came into this large room full of wall-to-wall mirrors and large black and white checkered flooring.

In the middle of the room stood a figure like I had never seen before. Bright green evening gown, feathers, flaming red hair, impossibly high heels all on an over six foot tall frame. The music blared as the entertainer slowly began to sway to the music. Bryant pulled me over to a table and I sat down without ever taking my eyes off the performer. I must have looked like Dorothy did when she saw the first flying monkey.

Strolling from one side of the floor to the other, slowly taking off one long silk glove, the tall wonder wrapped the glove around a young muscle bound boy in the front of the crowd and fake kissed his cheek.

Suddenly, Bryant leaned over to me.

"Man, these drag queens really know how to look like women!"

I blinked and stared at the performer again, my forehead wrinkling in concentration. He waited for my answer then noticed I had no idea what he was talking about.

"Drag queens. You know, guys dressed as girls."

He must have wondered at that point what the address was to the cave I'd been living in. I intensely studied the man who was now slowly unzipping the side of his gown.

But the makeup was perfect. And there were two lumps where the breasts should be. And where was his . . . you know, thing?

I looked around the room. How had I not noticed that it was crowded to the four corners with homosexuals? The space was full of men who were dressed and well manicured holding hands. Girls that I thought had been young boys in their ballcaps and oversized shirts were all around me. I turned to look behind me to see if there were any people like me. A beautiful, young girl smiled at me and waved a seductive little wave.

I didn't know what to do. I had been raised to believe that gay people were going straight to hell, were disease-ridden and if you spent time with them, apparently their gayness was contagious. Oh, and the possibility of contracting AIDS must be astronomical in this den of iniquity.

I looked at the plastic cup half full of the fruity drink I had taken a sip from expecting to see "drink me" written on the side and the Mad Hatter sitting down beside me and ordering another round.

This may seem odd but this is not the first time that I felt I had fallen down into a large, black hole full of odd creatures and unfamiliar surroundings. Let me take you back to the first day when I was three and a half and met my adopted family for the first time.

My social worker who called herself Miss Rose had shown up at the children's home full of bubbly excitement at my new placement. I, on the other hand, was not fully of bubbly excitement. Already jaded by being returned five times in four months, I was not falling for the "you're going to be our little girl" speech. One family had fostered me and apparently I was full of magic because the once barren mother was now pregnant and wanted to have her "own" child.

Another had two boys who were older than me but since I had taken care of myself since I was two, I ordered them around like a big sister. They thought that might be bad for their fragile male psyches. Another woman had become ill, and another family had decided to return to England.

I no longer cared. They called me "quiet" and "withdrawn" and no one asked me why that was. If they had, I wouldn't have told them about the man who had come into my room and crawled on top of me until I couldn't breathe and made odd grunting noises. Or the fact that my father had often forgotten to feed me as he sat in the bar below where we lived. Or that my dog was now living with my mom. Poor dog.

Miss Rose walked me down the stairs of the children's home and into the basement where both sides were lined with filing cabinets behind locked chain link fences. These cabinets were full of records of our real names and adopted names and who we were and who they decided we should become. An old cupboard stood at one side near the back of the room. Miss Rose opened the door and read aloud from a handwritten list taped to the inside.

"Let's see. . . girls age two to four. Okay, here we go. Four shirts, four pairs of pants . . . "

She grabbed a brown grocery bag from a bin nearby and began filling it with little girl clothes. I stood there and watched as yet another brown bag was packed with things I would need for yet another home that wouldn't want me. Miss Rose seemed to sense my "been here-done-this" attitude and stopped her packing.

"Marty, (that was my name before the adopted parents changed it at the age of 4) what say this time you pick out the shoes. Any pair you want. Just look them over and pick."

Having been given little to no say of anything in my life up to that point, the idea thrilled me. I walked over to the bin three rows down and looked at the collection. Miss Rose brought over a chair so that I could stand on it and see every pair. There were sneakers and lace up shoes. There were a few boots and even some slippers. But almost at once I saw them.

In the dim basement light, I saw a pair of shiny, black patent leather shoes with white, blue and pink stitching on top of them in the shape of a flower. As I leaned over to grab them, I could see my reflection in the toes of the polished material. I didn't even notice the slight scuff marks at the heel or the logo on the inside half worn off by wear. They were beautiful. They were mine.

Clutching the shoes to my chest, I looked over at Miss Rose, and saw her smile.

"Perfect choice."

I remember walking out of the double doors, with Miss Rose carrying my bag of clothes and me my shoes. I remember eating at McDonald's on our way to my new home. While I nibbled at a french fry, Miss Rose went on and on about how great this new family was going to be. I had heard it all before. I could have said it back to her.

"They have a son, so you'll have a big brother. Won't that be nice?"

I nodded as I sat with a hamburger in one hand and my shoes still clutched in the other. It must have looked odd to people around us but those shoes were my most treasured possessions.

Soon we pulled up to a small gray-sided house. Miss Rose put the car in park and turned to me.

"Marty, don't be scared. Just give it a chance. Smile, you are such a pretty little girl."

I liked her so I decided to somehow learn to smile in the next fifteen seconds. As we went up the flower-lined sidewalk, the front door opened. A woman with short brown hair stood there. The woman who would be my new mom....for however long it took to throw me back.

I disliked her instantly. Something about her eyes, her insincere smile. My survival alarms went off.

"Hi, there. Remember me? We met last week?" Her lips smiled but her eyes did not. I didn't remember her.

Whenever a potential adopted family where looking to adopt, they would clean us up and file us into the common room full of dark green plastic chairs and puke green linoleum. We would be forced to shake hands and talk. Sometimes I swear they would check our teeth like what someone does when they go to buy a horse.

I can't really describe what it is like to one day be home with both your parents, your mom walks out with your dog. Then another day, you are in a children's home and told you were taken away from your Dad because he was not fit to parent. Then a few other days of waking up with strange people in a strange house over five times. Then find yourself being stared out with over-friendly smiling adults who ask you a lot of stupid questions like "what your favorite color is" or "would you like to be our little girl", to eventually standing in the living room of yet another house with yet another smiling adult wanting you to call her "mom". There just aren't appropriate words in our dictionary for that.

But as the husband walked in, I felt my little frail body relax. His energy was safe. Maybe this home would be good. He shook my hand and I felt the calluses from honest hard work.

Suddenly, I sensed someone looking at me. It was a sixth sense that had stood me well in my young life of self survival. I turned and saw a chubby boy, Ricky, their son, standing there grinning from ear to ear. I smiled back with my slightly brown, bad teeth. My father's parenting technique had resulted in malnutrition, my hair falling out and bad teeth.

Within the next few days, these strangers insisted I call them "Mom" and "Dad", made me sit at a table and eat like a family, and pray to someone they called "Jesus" who apparently had to be talked to everyday or he would get angry. We also had to ask him to bless all our food. I didn't know if it made the food magical or better tasting.

They also kept calling me "Page". I kept informing them that I was "Marty."

The woman disagreed.

"It's Page now. Page Anne. That's the name we picked out."

I thought about that for a while and wondered if people were allowed to do that. Just decide to change someone else's name. It wasn't like I was a baby and would never know the difference. I mean wasn't it enough that I had to get use to a new home, new family, new town. I wasn't even allowed to keep my own name?!?

A few weeks later in exasperation after calling my new name a dozen times with me not responding, she called me "Marty."

Feeling I had proven my point well enough, I walked into the room and declared, "My name is Page".

It seemed to make her happy. That was about the last thing I did that pleased her in the 18 years I lived under her regime.

For the first few nights, I would sleep with my new shoes tucked under my chin to keep them safe, and would awake to the boy, my new older brother, staring down at me asking if I wanted to play. A couple of weeks later it sunk in that I was really there to stay. Apparently, I wasn't going anywhere and these people would have to be accepted and lived with. I began to sleep with my shoes under my bed but within arms reach in case I was sent packing.

So, I knew what it was like to feel that nothing was familiar and all was new and odd. I looked around the strip club and studied everyone. I studied Bryant's face as he talked to the girl-couple sitting at the table beside us.

Would he be this window into yet another new world? Or would he just throw me back as being the odd little girl who seemed uncomfortable in her own skin? I felt myself growing withdrawn and scared. I did snap out of it a little bit when I stared down at my red shoes…patent leather, shiny red shoes. Funny how you remember what shoes you were wearing when something important happens, or at least I can.

Five years later, I would walk away from him wiser, exhausted, more worldly. This artist named Bryant had hacked away at my marble frame making deep, lasting marks from what he called love. But what a world he had opened to me. And I felt ready to walk through it and discover who I really was. He had been a guide to things I had never read about or even heard about. Drugs, alcohol, my first orgasm, going backstage at rock concerts, being the girlfriend of a guy who played in a band.

Not to mention attending AA meetings with him, checking him in and out of rehab, rescuing him from habitual cutting and suicide attempts, restraining orders and being once again beaten.

Now, it was my time to walk alone awhile. I had walked with the light with Patrick and walked with the dark in Bryant. I was ready to stop falling down Alice's hole and begin this new journey down the yellow brick road alone.

And alone scared the shit out of me.

Note: As of this printing, Bryant has been sober almost 4 years!

FIVE

Person: Armagan

Lesson: Foreign men are amazing in bed.

Lesson: When you set a caged animal free, make sure it knows how to survive.

I need to give you a little bit of a timeline of "firsts" in my life.
First time I heard rock and roll - 18
First kiss – 18
First drink – 25
First cigar – 31
First orgasm (unassisted) – 30
First pair of jeans – 22
(Adopted Mom-ism…"ladies do not wear pants and Jesus said so.")
First time having sex – 24 *(wedding night)*
First time flying on a plane – 19
First time seeing the ocean – 18

First employment – 14

First time I saw a penis in real life - 22

First time seeing a black person– 18

First time allowed to cut my hair how I wanted, pierce my ears and wear makeup other then blush, and pick out my own panties that weren't briefs – 19 *(Adopted Mom-ism…"only whores wear thongs and eyeshadow")*

Age I had to grow hair back, throw away thongs and take off eye makeup - 19

First time allowed to shave above the knee – 16 *(Adopted Mom-ism… "why would you need to, no one sees above your knee since you wear skirts BELOW the knee unless you're doing something you shouldn't be.")*

So, now you know a little bit more about me and how utterly terrifying it was to have no one telling me what to do or how to do it. To be able to walk out of MY apartment door and DO anything. I was like one of those animals that is raised in captivity, and then taken back to the forest and the cage door is flung open revealing freedom.

However, unlike a deer being put back into the wild for the first time, there was no one there to gently urge me out of my comfort zone, and cry at the mere site of me running free.

I would literally sit or stand for hours in my apartment and wonder what I wanted to do. I had no clue even what I liked. Would I like to go get a martini and enjoy live music? What kind of martini do I ask for? What kind do I like? What kind of live music? Where would be a good place to hear live music? And what would I wear? What does one wear to a martini bar?

It would go on for hours and I would just sit there wishing that life in its infinite wisdom would have opened my cage door and instantly followed it with a nice tazer gun to my hindquarters so I would just run already. I would just sort of sit there and look around. Sounds and smells and shadows swirled around me while thoughts and questions and desires encased me in layers of uncertainty.

This went on for about six months. I know . . . that's sad.

Having left my husband, and a couple weeks later having had Bryant move in, I didn't make time for myself to discover who I was. Any good therapist worth her pay would have easily pointed out that Bryant had been a crutch because I had poured all my energy into keeping him alive while he helped me with my "daddy" issues. After all, my real father had picked alcohol over me, this man would see how amazing I was and I would win this time with his sudden sobriety, right?

But now I needed to stand alone. After my complete hysterectomy at the age of 32, I no longer had debilitating periods and constant pain but my moods were dictated by my lack of female hormones and I was going crazy.

The doctor put me on some anxiety medicine to help while going through early menopause. It had an interesting side effect…it cured shyness. I stopped feeling trapped in my own body and terrified of going to places I'd never been before. I had had this problem for so long, it was like the butterfly not pushing its way out of the cocoon but tearing through it.

When I was as a little girl in Ohio, the town was so small that it didn't even have a stoplight. There was a post office but it was in a lady's enclosed garage. There was one restaurant that we weren't allowed to go to because they served beer and we couldn't have anyone in the community thinking we supported alcohol. A nursing home where people from surrounding areas dumped their old. But in the center of it all where the two main streets intersected, there was a convenience store. It was a bare-bones setup, and on weekends outside in the dirt parking lot, the Amish would come, park their horse and buggies, and sell jams and jellies and brooms they had made. As children, we were allowed to go inside the store but only with permission. After all, they sold alcohol and cigarettes.

When I was about eight years old, Grams gave me fifty cents for dusting her house. My parents were very upset at this because we were not given allowances; we were expected to "earn our keep." Grams knew this but sometimes the short woman would draw herself up as tall as she could, tilt her chin, place one hand firmly on her hip, and just shake her head in silent protest.

She mistakenly thought she was doing me a favor by giving me money and insisting I go down to the corner store and buy candy with it so my mom wouldn't see that I had earned a small wage.

I walked down to the corner and stood outside the rusted out, bug covered screen door that led inside. I clutched the coins so tight in my hand that the president's face was pushed into my skin. I tried to see inside but the sun was too bright and the interior too dark. A breeze blew by causing a few dust swirls to rise off the ground and the smell of cigarettes wafted from inside.

I stood there and stood there. My feet wouldn't move. Cars drove by. People walked by. The black cat that no one owned but seemed to be the neighborhood's stopped and looked at me. I began to feel foolish and took a step forward, then another and reached for the door handle that was half hanging from a rusted bolt.

The door flew open and a man wearing a dirty baseball hat and overalls burst out. He paused and looked down at the odd little girl in her long skirt and plastic eyeglass frames too big for her small pale face. Her hands clenched into red little fists looking like she was going to faint. He smiled, turned and held the door open. I had no choice now. I had to go in.

I stepped inside and the door slammed closed behind me.

A voice came from the darkness,"Hello, little girl."

I don't remember running out of there but suddenly I was home and the two quarters were still in my hand.

As I went upstairs, I knew my mom would question where I got the money. I didn't want to get in trouble and I definitely didn't want to get my Grams in trouble. So, while my mom was busy hanging up the laundry in the back yard, I snuck into my parents' bedroom and tossed the coins into the pickle jar my dad kept for his change.

I stared at the quarters and decided I better shake the jar to make sure it wasn't obvious someone had contributed to it. My adopted mom had a photographic memory that was only good for knowing if someone had touched or moved anything. The best use of her talent was being able to catalog and critique who at church had worn what and what teenage girl was allowed to wear eyeshadow or who had hated God enough to wear pants to church.

I felt okay about my deposit as I walked out of the room. Felt like I had paid for my room and board for the day.

Each time I walked by that store, I would feel ashamed of myself. What was I so afraid of? Grams asked me what I bought and I lied and told her gum. She studied my face and because I always turned red when I lied, I knew she knew.

There was just something wrong inside of me that refused to let me go charging into the unknown. Maybe my young self being thrown into six homes in less then a year and being called a name that wasn't mine while being forced to be in a new family somehow wore out my sense of childlike adventure.

So, now in my 30's and armed with this new magical elixir known as Buspar, I began walking thru any door I wanted to. However, with this new found power came another small side effect . . . I found out I was desirable.

For some reason, men (I should say boys) who were a lot younger would hit on me. Being pale, never getting sun, and never getting drunk or smoking or anything normal people do in their 20's, I looked a lot younger than my age. When I was 32, I would constantly get carded for 21. I guess I can thank my biological mother for one thing . . .we age well.

I soon became almost drunk on the longing looks and invitations I would get from young men. I began to dress sexier and discovered stilettos. However, I didn't act on the constant come-ons. I just liked to accumulate them and later at night as I lay in bed play them over and over in my head.

Soon however, I discovered foreign men. Having grown up in the middle of Nowhere, Ohio, I had had very little interaction with foreigners. A few missionaries had come through our church who were not natives of the United States but that was about it. Being without a television almost my entire life, I had read of foreign places but had never heard a foreign language spoken.

While attending the Christian university, I had come more into contact with a few people not from here and had found their accents tickled my inner ear and awoke my imagination to a whole big world out there. I had, up until I was 29, only been to four other states but that was only to visit relatives. Never had I been abroad.

My best friend, Emily, and I were having dinner shortly after my third time breaking up with Bryant. The Italian restaurant was one of my favorites. I had slept with one of the waiters recently (well, we had gotten naked in the hallway of my apartment, fallen into bed and were well on our way to having sex when he suddenly bolted up, put on his clothes and said something about still being in love with his ex girlfriend). I waved to him as we were seated. Emily and I talked for a while about her newly started photography business and I talked about my graphic design company.

Then . . . he walked in.

He walked in and our table suddenly went mute. We both stared at him and I swear we both stopped breathing. Tall, lean with shoulder length black hair and dark eyes, he strolled . . .no, he walked as only foreign men can, by our table. Dressed in an obvious European fashion with black fitted pants, custom Italian shoes and a black button up shirt, he sat down and picked up a menu with fingers that were wearing beautiful silver rings. Even his thumbs were adorned.

Losing all maturity, Emily and I looked at each other and started to giggle. Yes, giggle. Our faces turned red. Then we started to laugh at the fact we were both giggling over a boy which made it continue on until the laughter tears started to fall and we had our hands up over our faces to cover our shame.

The waiter I had been naked with however briefly, walked over to his table. The foreigner began to speak and we leaned forward to hear. Was it a French accent? A British? What was it?

Having been friends for a while we didn't need to say words to have a whole conversation. Emily wrinkled her forehead and tilted her head while looking at me. I wrinkled my forehead and shook my head that I couldn't place the accent either. She reached up and stroked her long hair and shook her head in the affirmative that clearly meant she liked his hair. I nodded in agreement and smiled and pointed at myself. She nodded again and let me know that of course she knew I loved boys with long hair.

She could see him but I had the misfortune of having my back to him. I wanted to look at him too.

"Can I turn and look?" I asked her.

"No, he's . . .wait, okay, turn now." I whirled around and saw him studying the menu.

He was beautiful. Emily kicked me under the table and I realized I was still staring at him.

"God, he's….he's Orlando Bloom's prettier brother."

Emily agreed. "Damn."

"I wish we could take a picture without him knowing." Abruptly, Emily reached into her purse and pulled out one of her newly printed business cards I had designed for her. We had just been talking about her needing to expand her photography portfolio.

"I'm going to go ask him."

"For what?"

"To model."

"Really? Oh my god, really?"

Emily tapped the edge of the card against her lower lip as she studied him.

"Yes, I think…yeah, I think I will."

"Are you crazy? You're just going to go up and ask him?"

Instead of replying, she got up from the table and walked to his. As she talked to him, I felt my neck getting warm and my heart began to pound. I knew she was about to call me over. That's what good girlfriends do.

Sure enough she waved me over.

"Page, this is –I'm sorry, how do you say it again?"

"Armagan."

"Oh, R-ma-gan. Am I getting it right?" Emily asked with a laugh. He nodded in what seemed like a half bow and held out his hand to me. I shook it and glanced into his eyes feeling a few remnants of my shyness returning. Odd, it felt like his hand was shaking as well. He spoke so quietly you had to watch his lips to focus in on his words.

His lips. Damn. Beautiful vowels and consonants dipped in an accent that was soft and exotic swirled from his soft, full lips.

He told us he was from Turkey and was new to town. Emily asked him if he would pose for her. He let out the smallest of laughs.

"I do not model. I am a physicist."

Oh, god and he's smart too.

She soon convinced him it might be fun and why not? We shook his hand again and Emily gave him her card.

We returned to our table, sat and finished our meal. I was useless in engaging in conversation as I couldn't stop feeling him so close.

With my ears still pounding out the beats of my fast moving heart, we paid the bill, got up and walked outside. I completely forgot to say goodbye to the waiter. Damn, I probably couldn't have picked him out of a lineup at this point!

I am a little ashamed to say this but we actually stood outside talking until he came out. We waved goodbye to him and did the giggle thing again.

Sigh . . . no dignity.

They did the photo shoot two weeks later but I insisted I didn't want to come. At the time I was back living with Bryant again.

Honestly though, this foreign man with the perfect lips and the perfect hands and the perfect …everything scared me. It scared me how much I wanted him. All of him. I wanted those lips to whisper in my ear whatever he wanted to say in his native tongue. He could say what he bought at the grocery store for all I cared as long as it was his own language and his fingertips were brushing up and down my body.

We didn't see him again for two months. I had one of the photos that Emily took near my computer. She said he had been shy and awkward during the shoot but the three photos she sent me looked amazing. So, when I saw him again I immediately noticed he had cut about three inches off his hair and looked almost too slender. It wasn't bad. It was just like a famous painter who first revealed his masterpiece, and the second time a lesser-known piece but of the same undeniably beautiful subject.

So this night, shortly after another breakup with Bryant, and in one of those rare incidences when I could get Emily to come downtown, we were driving down Princess Street looking for parking. We drove by the venue where we were headed to hear our friends play music.

"Stop the car!" I yelled as I grabbed her arm.

"What?" she yelled back slamming on the brakes.

"It's him. Armagan. It's him! Isn't it?"

We both strained our necks to see. Emily ignored the car horn blaring behind us.

"Yeah, I think it is but he cut his hair. I don't know though. Let's find out."

Emily without asking permission began to simultaneously push the down window button on my side and honk her horn. He turned and looked.

"Hey, Armagan!" Emily yelled past my horrified face.

He stopped walking into the bar we would soon be going to and studied us. Thankfully, a look of recognition crossed his face.

"Hey, we'll be back soon. You going inside?" Emily continued to yell over the multiple car horns that were now sounding like an angry orchestra.

He smiled. "Yes, I will be in this place."

"We'll be there soon. Look for us!" Emily yelled.

As we drove on, I turned to look at Emily as she rolled my window back up and did a courtesy wave to the car behind us.

"Oh, stop looking horrified," she said. "You know you want to see him." Then without skipping a beat – "Man, I'm hungry."

She insisted she needed food or she would get one of her headaches. Unfortunately, she has never gotten over her mother's insistence that as a child she eat new things such as brussels sprouts and tuna casserole resulting in her only eating a caesar salad with grilled chicken when out of her home. The bar where the pretty boy was waiting did not have this on their menu. I hurried her to the nearest restaurant and pushed her to eat faster while in a decidedly unladylike way gulped down a cosmo.

"What if he leaves before we get there?" I asked.

"He'll be there. I need some more bread."

I swatted at her hand as she raised it to get the waiter's attention.

"You are literally killing me. You are going to make me slap you. In public. I am going to have to physically assault you."

"Fine," Emily smiled. "I was just messing with you. Let's go get you the pretty boy."

What seemed like hours later but was probably less then 15 minutes, we walked into the bar and there he was.

Emily grabbed my hand and walked me right up to him. He gave her a hug and shook my hand, introducing me to some guy standing beside him that to this day I couldn't tell you one thing about. He could have been introducing me to a leprechaun and I wouldn't have noticed.

I left to get drinks and while I was gone, Emily decided on her own to tell him that I liked him. (Something we had a LONG talk about later.)

He walked up to the bar and sat down beside me while the bartender poured my drinks. The band played loudly, the people talked louder around us and I could barely hear what he was saying let alone deal with his thick accent. A while later, tired of hearing almost every other word, and sure that he thought I was odd for staring at his lips for clarity (and the wanting to touch them with mine), I decided to lean in. So did he. He kissed me. Soft, slow. He pulled back and looked at me.

"Is this okay I did this?" he asked in a haunting accent.

I realized I had stopped breathing when I heard a loud sound of air being forced into my lungs. I smiled.

"Only if you promise to do it again."

Wow! Come on! That was a smooth line coming from the little Ohio girl. He smiled and did it again and again. An hour later, I was sitting on his couch in his apartment. He was playing Turkish music and I was surrounded by Turkish decorations. His Turkish cigarettes lay on the coffee table and he was in his kitchen making Turkish coffee. (So, yes, he is from Turkey.)

We talked for hours about his culture and where we grew up.

My "growing up" story seemed so monotonous compared to his stories of Istanbul and France and other exotic places. As the night was beginning to think about turning into day, he asked if he could read my coffee grinds. Apparently, it is a tradition that normally Turkish women do but a few men are trained in as well if they show any signs of having "the sight."

I handed over my now empty cup and he swirled the grinds a certain number of times and stared down at the message that awaited me. I stared at his amazing profile and wondered what kind of lover he would be.

"You have had sadness lately. It is over a boy, yes?"

I laughed. "That is too generic to prove you can see anything."

He squinted his eyes and you could tell he was thinking about a word I said that he didn't understand.

"Generic?" he asked and I explained. He nodded, ignored my disbelief, and looked back at the grinds. He quickly looked up again and then back down. Something bad?

"This boy has long hair and is very troubled. He has brought a lot of darkness to you. He has his own inner struggle and he is losing. And you are trying to break free of it."

I felt the room grow warm as I struggled to figure out how he knew Bryant. He had just arrived in North Carolina. Did we have mutual friends? No. Had he seen us out one night? No, I hadn't gone out with Bryant for a few months due to his rehab schedule. Was I about to accept the fact that he could see Bryant in the grinds?

I told him a little bit about Bryant and his addiction with alcohol and drugs, and my addiction to him. He nodded like he already knew.

As the sun was coming up, he laid me in his bed. It was just like those covers you see on the front of romance novels coming to life. He was passionate and sure. He was tender and powerful. When we were done, he began to run his fingers along my neck, hips, thighs and breasts whispering the Turkish word for each in my ear.

We would be lovers over the next year but never a couple. It wasn't a good time for either of us. I think there was a part of me that didn't want to date him. I wanted him to stay that mysterious man with the accent that I lusted after for two months. I didn't want to start dating him and begin to know his faults and he mine. I never wanted the beauty of him to fade. I wanted the masterpiece to never lose its color.

So, we became friends with amazing benefits. We would even talk about other people we were sleeping with. We'd meet for brunch or for a drink. I'll never forget the time he brought me medicine and soup when I had a cold, put me to bed and while rubbing my back, he sang a Turkish lullaby to me until I fell asleep.

His company sent him to Japan for three months and we talked everyday on the phone. A few times, he called me late at night and woke me up. He insisted on singing me back to sleep with Turkish songs or he would whisper children's stories or fables that he had heard as a child.

I think back about that little girl who was so scared that she couldn't walk into that store in that small town in Ohio. I felt sad because I wondered how many other amazing people I would have met and known, and lands I would have been able to discover, if as a child, I had learned to just walk through that screen door.

SIX

Person: Alex

Lesson: There is no easy way to find out you are bisexual

Lesson: Sexually repressed Fundamentalist mothers should never give the sex talk.

One day when I was ten, a cardboard box came in the mail addressed to me. I never got mail so it was pretty exciting.
Inside was a free sample of a tampon. My mother's face went from horror to contemplation to resignation. So, she sat me down and gave me the "birds and bees" talk.

Of course, my adopted mother gave "the talk" with her own twist. Her mother had given it to her with her own twist as well. On my grandmother's wedding night, grandpa stuck his penis in her and she wasn't sure why. She continued to wonder why for over 40 years.

My mom's twist is that when she was little, she and her brothers were swinging in the barn on one of the large metal hooks that were used for moving bales of hay. She lost her grip and slid down it causing the hook to go inside of her vagina. She lost most of the sensation in that area from that point on.

"So, when a man and a woman are married, they have what is called 'sex'."

I looked at her with no understanding. She picked up the box and began tapping the edge of it on the kitchen table.

"Do you know how moms get pregnant?"

I thought about it and gave her my best guess.

"I guess it's because they kiss on the mouth and use the same toothbrush?"

My mother snorted and rolled her eyes. I felt very stupid.

She began tapping more rapidly as words that didn't seem comfortable in her mouth spilled out.

"No, it's when a man takes his penis –"

"What's a penis?" I asked.

"It's what God gave a man, you know down there. He puts it in your vagina—you know what that is, right?"

I nodded that I did know if she was referring to that hole down there. I went to a Christian school my whole life so it wasn't like we had sex education classes or even anatomy classes of any kind.

"Well, he puts his—his penis inside of you and stuff comes out that can make you pregnant. It's called semen and you have eggs. They combine to make a baby."

I studied on that for a while wondering how I never knew I had so much in common with a chicken.

"So, every time he puts it there it happens?" I asked.

"No, not every time. Just sometimes."

"So you have to practice?"

"No, it's just sometimes you just do it to feel good. It feels good to the man. It's your duty as a wife to let him do it. You must honor and obey your mate. Like the Bible says."

I suddenly pictured my mom lying with her long skirt up around her hips and my father sticking his thing inside of her, squirting something while she read the Bible until he was done. Maybe even patting him on the head as he rolled off of her. I didn't think it sounded like anything I was too interested in.

"Now in a couple of years you'll get your period. I don't get one anymore because I had a surgery and they took all the female parts out. But you will and that is what this is for."

She opened the box and out fell a white cylinder.

"Now, put that away until you need it. You'll get a period once a month and you'll have blood come out from between your legs. It's natural. You'll get cramps first. It's like a stomachache only lower. It's the curse we got from Eve being weak and sinning when she ate the apple. Your period stops once you get pregnant until you have the baby."

"But why do we have to be punished for something Eve did? That doesn't seem fair."

"Well, Eve was weak and did something God told her not to. The curse He put on her was a curse on all women."

I picked up the tampon and studied it then decided that when I got to heaven, I would find Eve and promptly punch her in the face.

My older brother, Ricky walked into the kitchen to get a drink.

"What are you talking about?" he asked.

My mother told him we were talking about the birds and the bees. He stood and chewed on his fingernails like he always did when pondering something.

"I still don't get how that works."

Very rarely in the years I had lived with them had I seen my adopted mother grow frustrated with her precious, precious son. They had almost an unhealthy love for each other, kissing hello and good-bye on the mouth. The boy could do no wrong in her eyes. He was "the good child".

However, as she turned to look at him I heard a big sigh that was normally only reserved for me, and a look of pure frustration cross her face.

"Ricky, I've told you three times, your father and I together have told you twice. You are 13 years old. What don't you understand?"

"Uh, I guess all of it. What makes her get a baby?"

Happy that for once I was the more intelligent child, I decided to step in.

"When you put your penis inside her vagina and stuff comes out and she gets pregnant."

My mom turned and looked at me with some sense of horror that I had understood sex before her bright, baby boy. Oh, and the fact that the word for male genitalia was now sounding so natural to me.

"Oh, and she bleeds every month from her lady parts until you get her pregnant."

"Ewwwwwww….." my brother exclaimed.

He walked on over to the fridge having suddenly lost interest in the whole thing. My mom sighed heavily again and mumbled, "I don't think he'll ever get it," before walking out and leaving me to play with the tampon.

At the age of 12 when I got my period and because she is who she is, my mother suddenly started stalking my every movement when out of her sight.

She didn't come right out and say my biological mother was a whore (to do that, she would have to break her "I don't know anything about your parents" innocence) but throughout my life, she treated me like at any moment I would be turning tricks on the corner now that I could pregnant so she must be hyper-vigilant.

I got my period in the middle of Sunday morning church that is yet another early-onset sign that God didn't much care for me. I went to the bathroom, saw blood and cried. The pain was unbelievable and it never got better until I had a hysterectomy in my 30's.

When I was in my sophomore year of college, I fainted from the pain of my endometriosis. I was unconscious for over fifteen minutes, and an ambulance was called. It happened a lot, I would be standing in the kitchen doing dishes and my mother would hear a thud behind her. I'd come to, get up, and continue working.

"Are you okay?" she would ask.

"Yep."

My close friends were use to it but they always acted like it was a big thing. Bringing me water, a cool towel. You know, the things a real mom would do.

This time it happened at work. Fifteen minutes was a long enough time that my coworkers had panicked and called 911. I was rushed by ambulance to the ER, the whole time insisting they stop and let me out.

At the hospital, I asked the nurse to call my boyfriend, Rob, at the time but he was in class. I then said to call my father. Somehow the nurse interpreted that to mean to call my mother.

Shortly after the call was made, another nurse with long blonde hair and a smiley face pin on her collar walked in and explained that my mother would be in shortly.

"Please don't let her in. I'll be fine. It's really not necessary."

The nurse adjusted the pin on her uniform to the appropriate full smile position, and with a very similar smile as the pin informed me it would be fine. A girl needed her mother.

"Uh, no. I don't. Really. I'm an adult. I can handle this myself."

And then there she was in her long-skirted, sour-faced glory.

"I can't believe I'm losing work over this. I'm going to have to make up the time. I'll probably have to work through lunch. And why would you want to drag your father out of his job to spend time here? It's not like you're dying. You look fine to me. Now Judy is going to have to work through her lunch and then Brenda will have to stay late. And do you have any idea how much money an ambulance costs?"

She whirled to face the unsuspecting nurse. "How long do you think this is going to take?"

The nurse stopped moving around the room and was staring in horror at my mother. The pin was now definitely shifting towards being upside down again and more appropriately so.

The nurse was spared when the doctor walked in and introduced himself to us. He sat down and pulled out a clipboard and began to ask a checklist of questions. My mother was surprisingly quiet until the doctor got to the checkbox asking if I could be pregnant.

"Could this be because you are pregnant? Sometimes in early stages of pregnancy fainting can happen." He turned to me. "Could you be pregnant?"

I, horrified, shook my head. "I've never had sex."

The doctor noted it on the sheet of paper.

"What if she had had sex?" My mother asked.

The doctor continued to scribble and said without looking up, "She said that she hasn't."

"But what if she had. Would you need to do a test on her? A pregnancy test?"

The doctor looked up and studied my mother. "To help rule out why she is fainting and suffering such pain in her abdomen and ovaries, we would normally run a pregnancy test and a panel of STD tests as well. I don't see a need for that here."

"Run them. Give her the tests."

"Ma'am, she is over 18. She can refuse the tests."

But I knew what that would mean to her. It would prove I wasn't a virgin and that I thought I might be pregnant and possibly have an STD (whatever that was). I knew this woman. He didn't.

"Do the tests." I said.

As I laid back and let him do the pelvic exam, I cried because it hurt, I cried because I was ashamed and I cried because I realized that no matter how good a girl I was, it would never measure up to being anything. She would always see me the way she saw me.

So after I had my hysterectomy almost three years after my marriage was over, the periods stopped, the pain stopped and guess what? I started to like sex.

I began to learn what I liked and disliked in the bedroom. I discovered oral sex and different positions. Yes, the good Christian girl learned more then the missionary position. I soon began to know what to ask for, what to do and how to do it. I even watched porn for training.

But one night changed me and a label was soon slapped on me . . . bisexual.

As I spent more and more time downtown in restaurants and bars, I began to notice something. Girls love to kiss me. They would just walk up and lay one on me. And I liked it.

The first girl I slept with was my next door neighbor, Brittany. And yes, when I go in, I go all in . . . she was a stripper.

Bryant and I had loved to go to strip clubs. Before the night was over, we would have four or five of the girls just sitting around our table sometimes buying us drinks. We became friends with some of them, listening to either their hard life stories, or watching them trying to remember if when they went to Wal-mart if they had gotten the diapers needed, or whose boyfriend had hit them, or who was in rehab with a coke problem.

One of the first times we went to the local club, one of the cocktail waitresses was walking us to a table when we heard someone yelling at us from the pole.

"Hey, neighbors! Hey!" Brittany stood there in nothing but her g-string enthusiastically waving causing her large fake breasts to move side to side. That was her, one of the most innocent, fragile, sweet girls to ever strip.

The first time Brittany and I slept together, Bryant and I had broken up again so she and I decided to go out for a girls night. We had dinner then went to the strip club. Afterwards, we decided to have a drink at my place.

As we walked in, she slammed me against the wall and began to kiss me. We ended up in the bedroom where she went down on me and it felt so odd that a girl was down there that I faked a fast orgasm. I decided it was only polite to return the favor but once down there, it smelled odd and I really didn't know what I was doing. I ended up using my finger until she came, then we fell asleep.

The next time we did it, we did a threesome with my then current lover, Darron, but that did not go well. Darron was a fireman who I had met at the strip club after the final breakup with Bryant now back in rehab.

One thing that porn or even erotic movies do not show you is that it is very important to set guidelines in place when doing a threesome. Trust me.

This is how my first threesome went.

I made out with Brittany with Darron watching. Darron and I had sex with Brittany helping out. Then they had sex. A long session of sex.

I went to get some water. Came back in. They were still going. Left. Came back. Figuring if I stayed and watched any longer they might charge me admission to the show, I left again.

While listening to them from the next room, I discovered that I really liked Darron and didn't enjoy this after all. Almost forty minutes later, he emerged sweating profusely and asked where I went. I said I got bored watching them and maybe I should just leave. He apologized and hugged me. I pulled away.

"I guess I just figured out I like you." I told him.

His face lit up.

"I like you too. I figured this is what you wanted."

"It was but now . . . it isn't."

He kissed me then jumped up and told me he would shower and then take Brittany home. Then we could have a long talk.

He went to jump in the shower and on the way by the bedroom, informed Brittany it was time to go.

She rushed out of the room with the sheet wrapped around her, took one look at my face and burst into tears.

"You're the only girlfriend I have! Don't hate me! I'm so sorry. Ple—ea—se don't haaaaate me!" She wailed.

I couldn't calm her down.

"It's not your fault. I just figured out I like him, and you seemed to be enjoying yourself pretty loudly and Darron was enjoying himself a lot. And it felt like I was the third wheel and —"

"But I didn't even come!" she yelled. "I was just making noise so he'd feel good and keep him going for when you came back!"

I tell you, if they gave Oscars for faking an orgasm, this girl would have trophy cases stacked with them.

"Really?"

"Yeah, he's not even that good. It kinda hurt a little but I thought I should keep going because I thought you were coming back and I wanted to keep him going for you, but it wasn't good. He just sorta pounds at you."

We hugged it out. As I leaned back and we smiled at each other, I saw Darron standing behind the couch with a towel wrapped around his waist with a look of great dismay. It took a little convincing to get him to feel good about himself again but eventually he did.

After that first threesome, Brittany and I slept together a couple more times but it never really felt normal.

I've known but not acknowledged my whole life that I was drawn to girls. From the first time I masturbated, I would think of a girl's body.

Actually, my best friend, Wendy, on a sleep over at her house around the age of 11 taught me how to masturbate.

"If you put your fingers right here, and rub it, it feels good. Really good," she explained. "My mom says it's completely natural." Since her mom was my mom's best friend since high school, I felt it would be adopted-mom approved.

"Right here?"

"Yeah, try it."

We laid side by side and both in total innocence did it. Yes, she was right. It did feel really good.

I would think of boys but it never worked. When I thought of women, their skin, their warmth, their lips, their breasts . . . it worked quite well.

However, seeing as my parents told us that all homosexuals were an abomination to God and all would surely burn in hell for all eternity, and then attending the Christian university who would kick you out if you were gay or even had gay friends, it wasn't something I explored.

So, a few years later after Brittany, I had kissed about a dozen girls, slept with two of them involving threesomes but never with anyone like . . . Alex.

Ohhhhhhh, Alex.

The moment I walked into my favorite restaurant and saw her behind the bar setting out glasses, I wanted her. You know how when cartoon characters smell something they like and their noses twitch and they dance on their tippy-toes while following after a swirling mist of scent above them? Yeah, it was like that.

She was a perfect mix of lesbian. Her hair was cut short but had long bangs in the front that were streaked with a blonde section that showed up against the brunette part. Her hips were perfect and her neck was graceful. There was something about her that you just wanted to watch. She had a kind of awkward confidence, a sort of harmless beauty that if you exposed yourself to enough would swallow you up.

She smiled at me as I walked up to the bar to sit down. I introduced myself and she shook my hand. I remember consciously thinking to myself "let go of her hand, moron, let go of her hand" in that inner voice that sounds just exactly like my adopted mother's.

I watched her move back and forth. Studied her body. Her movements were boyish but not butchy. And her accent . . . it was thick with Southern dialect. Her phrasing and pacing different than I had heard before. She was loud when she talked which is something I normally hate but with her it just kind of didn't matter. I was mesmerized.

Fearing I was staring too much, and with the current boy I was sleeping with texting me wondering where I was, I forced myself to leave. She waved goodbye. I sighed as the door closed behind me wishing I could just stay.

A week or so later, I had a huge fight with James (the current lover) at the pool house, and since it was right next door to the restaurant that I loved, I walked in. Fuming I sat down and ordered a glass of wine, no, make it a double jack and diet.

I looked down the bar and there she was sitting on a one of the tall bar stools. She motioned me over. She could tell I was upset and as I approached her, she held out her arms and without hesitation I walked into them. She pulled me in between her legs and wrapped her arms around me. Having heard me tell her fellow bartender my current distress, she held me in a kind of "sisterhood, unite!" type of hug.

I could feel the warmth of her breasts against mine, the heat coming from her inner thighs. I wanted to stay there. She kissed me on the cheek and I hoped she didn't notice the smallest of sniffs I gave to her neck.

Another week went by and one of my client's took me to dinner there. While I was waiting for him, she walked out of the back kitchen and right up to me and hugged me. I didn't want her to let go. Not caring if I came across as needy or creepy, I held on a little too long.

Still waiting for the client, the wait staffs changed from the lunch crew to the dinner crew all the people I knew filed out. The chef gave me a hug, the server a kiss on the cheek, the manager a handshake.

Then she walked by. Just . . . walked by. I was crushed. You know that feeling you used to get when your class in elementary school would exchange Valentines with each other and the boy you liked the most didn't give you one? Like that.

Being my usual sarcastic self, I yelled after her.

"It's okay. Leave. It's not like we're friends or anything."

She stopped, turned around and smiled. Then without a moment of hesitation, she walked right up to my table, swiveled my chair around, leaned in and kissed me softly but firmly on the mouth.

I remember kissing her back and then thinking I should kiss her back. Okay, I got flustered. It had been awhile since I felt that flush spread over my face. She saw it and laughed as she walked out.

The next time I saw her I had ended it with James and she was ending her shift.

"Let's go get a drink somewhere, okay?" She asked in that drawl that was both endearing and sexy.

"Ok. Sure. Lead the way."

She grabbed my hand and as natural as if we'd been together forever, we started walking down the sidewalk. Well, in this small downtown, the cat would be out of the proverbial bag now. Everyone knew she was a lesbian and several lesbians always were swirling around her wherever she went. She had a reputation for turning straight girls gay. She was sort of like the "it" lesbian in our town.

As we passed bars with doormen I knew and we went to bars full of bartenders and bar backs I knew, I discovered I was out. Not outside out but gay out.

A few drinks later, at a bar called the Elixir Room, we were holding hands and kissing and dancing and laughing. It was odd for me, not because she was a girl but because I caught myself just being me. Also, oddly, I didn't care if people were watching us. It felt comfortable and exciting at the same time.

As we wondered from one bar to the next, I mocked her for the ability to take ever word that was one syllable and make it more then one due to her Southern accent.

She smiled and said "shiiiiiiiit, gurl. I do-oo no-oot."

Later that night as she made me realize what I had been missing by not having sex with a completely committed lesbian, I finally understood something. I was bisexual. I did like men and was attracted to them but when having sex with them it was more about seeing that they wanted me or for them to think I was good in bed. With girls, it was about . . . being in the moment. Although it took me a few times to get to that stage. Oh, let's be honest, I'm still working on it.

As we lay naked in the bed and her mouth was on my breasts, she suddenly stopped.

"Guuurrrl, what are thinking so hard on?"

I lifted my head to look at her. "What?"

"I can hear you thinking. Rela-a-a-x. Stop thinkin' so damn much."

With her, I began to stop thinking so much. To just feel. Feel comfortable in my own body. Also, it isn't like when men do foreplay solely so you'll reward them by letting them have sex with you (even if they bother to do foreplay at all). Sleeping with a woman is all foreplay.

Who better to understand how a woman likes to be kissed on her neck or how amazing it feels to have a warm tongue follow the curve of your hip than another woman?

The next morning as I woke up I felt her naked body against mine. Her skin soft and smooth. Her breathing slow and steady. Her hair covering her eyes. I put my arm around her and felt her breasts against my hand as I slid it to place it on her hips. She reached down and grabbed my fingers, softly moaned, and held them tight.

I had gone from sex being painful, to not knowing how to have sex, to learning how to, and now to this point. Later, as I told one of my friends what had happened over a Mimosa and an omelet, he declared that I was now gay.

"Why?"

He took a long drink from his glass. "You have to pick. You're either straight or gay."

I felt confused. I know I'm from backwoods country but I was pretty sure that I had understood the definition of "bisexual".

"Why can't I be both?"

"Because if you like girls, then you're a lesbian. If you like guys, you're straight. Oh, and lesbians don't like bi-girls. It frustrates them."

"Really? Huh, I had no idea. I thought I'd just be myself. I'm bisexual."

It felt good to say it out loud. Like I finally got an answer correct on a test that I had taken time and time before.

"Nah, you can't be bi. You can be but that means you are gay."

Apparently with him straight or gay were my two options. Please check the appropriate box. Pick one flag and fly it.

I thought about it. Was I now a lesbian? Did I have to join some kind of club or know a secret handshake? Was there a whole new culture I would have to acclimate to? Were there more doors I would have to walk through? Was I about to go yet again down into Wonderland?

More importantly, would I need a whole new wardrobe???

SEVEN

Person: Jackson

Lesson: Always find out the age of the boy you are taking home.

Lesson: It's never too late to find out you are not ugly.

So I now found myself in my late 30's and once again alone. Husband, gone. Rock and roll boyfriend, gone. Home, gone. Money, gone. Job, gone. Me . . . gone?

I caught myself thinking about one of those crime shows where the woman disappears and they interview those who knew her about what they think happened.

They would interview my ex-husband.

"She probably went to find herself . . . again. Maybe she's lost herself and went to go find out where she left herself. I'm not quite sure . . . but it did involve traveling . . . I think."

Of course, Bryant would be interviewed in yet another rehab facility, shaking like a cold Chihuahua and chain-smoking out an explanation of why he should have been a rock god.

My adopted mother, with my adopted father sitting dutifully quiet beside her, would assume . . . " She has probably gone to doing drugs or prostitution. I mean, we did the best we could but that girl always had the Devil in her." Insert dramatic sigh.

Then they would start flashing those pictures of you with unfortunate hair and eyeglass choices. And that's when it hit me. I immediately picked up my phone and called my best friend, Emily.

"Hey, darling! What's up?" she asked.

"If they ever do a TV show on me from when I die, you know, if something bad happens to me, I need good pictures."

This is how you know you have a good friend. A friend that understands and who accepts you as you are, and thankfully is a photographer.

"Sure. When you want to do it?"

That weekend, I dressed up in a black dress and pumps and we wandered around downtown near my loft apartment looking for locations. We did a few test shots by an old church to warm up. After about 50 shots, she broke down under my constant whining of not getting to see the pictures and showed me one.

I couldn't believe it. That wasn't me. Couldn't be. I was beautiful. Strong looking. Even almost thin and my breasts looked perky. My eyes exuded sexuality. I looked better now then I did in my 20's! What had happened?

Now, before you think I am terribly vain, you have to understand that like most women, I come from a long line of self-deprecation solidified by a "you'd look good if your stomach didn't pooch out" constant comment from my adopted mom, acne that decided to attack my senior year of high school, hormone treatments in my 20's that made me gain 48 pounds, the always popular "oh, you know Page, the girl with glasses" description, and the one that stuck in my head the most . . . the time when I was 13 and walking to my grandparents and three boys in a pickup truck howled at me like a dog, barking and laughing and calling me something to do with a canine.

And now, after losing weight, getting contacts, using dermatologist approved medicine, and getting all my painful girl parts taken out, I had emerged a very odd mixture of high self esteem bordering on pride, and low self-esteem bordering on shyness.

Having gone to Christian schools my whole life, we were never allowed to date or be alone with the opposite sex. For the majority of my life, I went to a church that was held in our pastor's living room and had about three families as the congregation. With this group came certain restrictions on young women of impeccable virtue.

No makeup, no short hair, no pants, no swimsuits (we had to swim in culottes and t-shirts. I almost drown during lifeguard training camp that was held in a nearby lake because my culottes were so wide so as not to show off my thighs that they got tangled up in some underwater moss and grass and I couldn't get loose), no plucking your eyebrows, no shaving your legs above your knees, no dangling earrings (only small clip ons with pearls or such, as pierced ears were a sin), no blouse or shirt could be lower then 2 finger lengths below your collarbone, no skirt could be higher then your kneecap while sitting, definitely no jeans and for Jesus' sake, no padded bras. Although, there was one time a year that the preacher's four daughters were allowed to wear pants under their skirts . . . during deer season while up in their tree stands.

So being thought of as beautiful or sexy was never even considered. In tenth grade, a boy named Jeff told me I was pretty. I remember looking down at my school jumper with the wide collar and flat chest and wondering what he meant.

Now I think back and like most of us women, I would kill for that body, that weight, and that skin that I had then. But I didn't see it, (sigh) we never do.

And now, here I was at 36 years of age and finally, setting all modesty aside, I was actually pretty. Okay, I'll say it . . . even sexy.

Thus began what I like to call "my slut years."

I would dress up on a Friday night, go out by myself, and hunt. I'd start at the French restaurant downtown and sip a glass of red wine surveying the crowd. By the second glass, I'd start to feel friendly maybe speak to the couple beside me or flirt with the bartender. Then I'd go to the martini bar or the wine shoppe and just talk. Listen to my friends play in their various bands of rock, soul, jazz or funk. Sit and gossip with the bar backs or owners of clubs. And because I was by nature (or should I say as a result of my lack of nurture) and thanks to Buspar, a friendly person who loved to hear people's stories, it wasn't long before I knew everyone and had many friends and more exciting, many friends with benefits.

It was amazing. I didn't have to date someone or listen to them talk about their lives or mine, or even (hold on!) know their names! I just walked thru the jungle of downtown like a lioness pausing to mate with whomever I chose. I could walk into any place, find whom I wanted to take home, and they would come. I became drunk on their words of how beautiful I was, how much they wanted me, had watched me downtown and wanted to be with me. They loved my hair, my eyes, my clothes, my shoes, my sense of humor, and my sexiness. I became what few women feel before the age of 40 . . . comfortable in my own skin.

Soon, I had three regular friends with benefits. My girlfriends couldn't keep them all straight when I talked about them so we gave them nicknames. There was 6'4", not terribly creative because he was actually that height. There was the "Cop," again because he was one, and the "Chef" again, he was.

We would call whenever one of us was horny and we'd have sex and then they'd either stay or leave. It worked very well because I didn't have to put the effort into hunting every weekend. They thought I was amazing too because I didn't care if they slept with other people or would disappear for a couple of weeks at a time. I made no demands and they in turn made none. It was perfect.

There are two lovers that sort of define the beginning and the end of this time in my life. One was Charles. He was at the end.

He had long hair and amazing eyes. He worked in my favorite wine bar called Morgan's. I went there at least two or three times a week because I was friends with the bartenders and soon became friends with the staff. I would bring my clients in there during the week and tip them well, and during slow times before the weekend crush, I would sit and hear about their breakups and financial problems and whatever else they wanted to talk about.

Charles would often stand quietly at the end of the bar with a well-worn book in his hand and chew on a straw. His apparent lack of noticing me at first miffed and then intrigued me.

It took about three weeks for him to talk to me. He had spent his formative years in the Sudan where his father worked for the Army. He had that confidence that people who have lived in different cultures have but maintained the shyness of a man who didn't feel like he quite fit in here either.

He told me he was at the end of his shift and asked if I wanted to come over to his house for a drink. Of course I said, yes. We walked in and poured some wine and then went to sit out on his back deck. The stars were out and it was a bit cold.

Not much for words, I tried to get him to tell me about himself. It was odd. It started out as this small wave of where he was from and how many brothers and sisters, and gradually grew to this tidal wave against American culture and academics, to a hurricane of the ignorance of organized religion and the stupidity of the broken dream of democracy.

I was stunned. I listened to him for hours. He would smoke and refill our glasses and eventually he lit candles so we could see each other, as the night grew darker and darker. Finally, he saw me shiver and led me inside to get warmed up.

As he walked down the hallway to get a blanket off of his bed, I followed him and he stopped. I leaned up against the back of him, my arms reaching around to hold him. I felt his breath catch. Slowly, he turned to face me and I kissed him. He responded at first like he didn't know where his lips should go. He fumbled a little barely brushing his bottom lip against mine. I wondered if it was possible this was a first kiss for him? Or maybe he was just nervous or——then he kissed me. And I realized that when someone wants to kiss you and remember all the taste of you and smell of you and breath of you . . . they kiss you like this.

Throughout the rest of the night, he moved slowly but with deliberation and passion. It was like feeling your body float in warm water. He took his hair out of the ponytail holder he always wore it in and it cascaded down onto my face in soft curls. It smelled of cigarettes, cologne and warm skin.

The next morning he made coffee and I left to go to work. I

couldn't get over how my body felt that day. I would catch myself at work sitting with my eyes closed remembering every moment.

Two days later, I went back to Morgan's with clients and we pretended that it was all business as he waited on our table. Later that night, he text "again?"

Of course, I said yes and spent another amazing night. Then a couple of days later, I text him to meet me at the martini bar and I'd buy him a drink. He text back, "can't. I can't get in."

I wrinkled my forehead over that and text back wanting to know what he meant. He text back what he meant and as I stared at my phone screen I stopped breathing.

"I can't. I'm not 21."

Oh . . . . dear . . . lord . . .

I had not only robbed the cradle but apparently I had robbed the cradle, dismantled it and burned it. I text him back with shaking fingers the next obvious question.

"How old are you?"

I waited and prayed that his answer didn't end in -teen. The couple beside me gave me a look and I realized I was loudly tapping my fingernails on the polished bar while awaiting his answer.

"20 yrs. old, silly, LOL. I thought you knew."

Okay, the cradle was still in one piece but there was a possibility that at 36 I would still get a one-way-go-to-the-front-of-the-line ticket to hell. One thing was for damn sure; I would have to start asking people's ages before taking them to bed.

He was an amazing lover for his age. He seemed to know what the female body needed and how to make it beg for him to be inside. He would get me so turned on until I begged him to be inside of me.

There was only one problem. He could not ever bring himself

to initiate sex. He told me it had always been a problem and that girls had broken up with him over it in high school. One even thought he was gay.

So one night as he played his records on his turntables and mixed up some dj effects, wearing earphones and boxers and nothing else, he set out a challenge.

"Let's make a bet, I bet that you can't name the next song I play."

"Okay, what do I have to do if I lose?"

"You make dinner and clean my apartment wearing only a bra and panties."

"And if I win? Oh I know, you have to initiate sex. Are you sure about this song choice?"

He laughed. "Having you ask me if I've ever heard of a band called Aerosmith last week, I feel pretty safe. Here, I'll try and go easy on you."

We shook on it and I resumed my position under the table and listened.

Unfortunately for him, he picked one of the only Pearl Jam songs I know.

His face looked terrified. I reminded him he was a man of his word. He agreed but wandered out of the room and into the hallway. He stood there between the music room and his bedroom like he had just lost his way and needed directions through his own home.

I patiently walked over to him and stood within arms reach. Minutes went by and he continued to just stand there. I wondered what had happened to him in the past to make him so scared of that first step.

I reached out my hand, patted his arm and began to walk towards the front door.

"It's okay. It was just a silly bet—"

He pounced. There really is no other word for it. He grabbed me from behind, swung me around and kissed me like very few times in my life I have been kissed.

He kept his lips on mine as he began to undo my jeans and lead me into the bedroom.

From that moment on, he never hesitated again.

We were together for almost three months. Actually, it was the three months that Armagan had been sent to Japan for work. I told Charles that he was coming back to the United States the following week and suddenly, he began to feel jealous and decided with great finality to tell me he never wanted to see me again. And he was gone.

I missed him a lot but understood. Even in his youth, he knew he couldn't expect me to settle down and besides, how much longer could a boy starting in his 20's and a woman hurtling towards 40 have anything in common?

To this day, I have rarely ever had such a moment as we had in that hallway. It's one of those memories that when you close your eyes and think of it, your whole body starts to tingle.

I saw him again recently when he began working at the new wine bar downtown. I was with a couple of girls and they went on and on about how gorgeous he was, and his long hair, his body.

"Isn't that guy sexy as hell? I bet he's good in bed."

I grabbed the glass of wine in front of me while I travelled back in my mind once again to the hallway. I smiled.

"I bet he is", I said.

EIGHT

Persons: Rapists

Lesson: There are way too many things to plan when you want to commit suicide

Lesson: No one and no act done to you defines who you are.

So there is something I didn't tell you about my biological father that I guess I should go ahead and tell you now since this needs a bit of information to help explain itself.

Among the many things that I discovered about my beginnings soon after my father died, was that when my father and I lived above a bar when I was around the age of two and a half, he would often get drunk with me at the bar.

I would sit there as a quiet little girl of all of two years of age, and watch him drink. My meals consisted of peanuts from the bowls on the table or whatever food the bartenders brought me. The owner of the bar let my father and I live above this establishment in exchange for my father cleaning the place, sweeping the floors, and taking out the garbage.

So my father had no real money to spend and when he got on the bad side of that night's bartender, the free drinks would stop. This is when apparently, he would put some music in the jukebox and set me on top of the table and have me dance for money for the other men at the table.

This would go on until I fell asleep in one of the booths and the staff would carry me upstairs to bed. Now you know why the bartender took it upon himself to call child services.

What I am going to tell you next brings with it the greatest shame and anger of my life but not the way you think.

When I was small and in my newly adopted home, I began to have nightmares. I would be asleep and hear a noise. I would wake up and see that I was sleeping in a bunk bed with the covers wrapped tight around me. A creaking of a doorknob would break the silence and I would turn my head to see a sliver of light as the door slowly opened.

I saw the outline of a large creature, dark and menacing. It walked thru the door and something bright around it's neck flashed into my eyes. I tried to move but I was tucked in too tightly. His large silhouette filled the floor as the creature walked over to the bed and slowly lay down on top of me. I felt like I couldn't breathe as the weight became more and more. Then the covers slowly moved off of me and I could feel his fur on my stomach. He began to softly growl and I was terrified. Then I felt pain near my stomach but lower. I looked up and felt warmth breath on my face that smelled of something I wasn't familiar with. Just beyond his left ear, I suddenly could see some stars. I focused on them and soon I felt my body floating up above the body in the bed, racing towards the stars. I would wake up crying silent tears and feeling like my stomach was still floating.

As the years went on, I would have that dream more and more often but details began to become more clear. The bear became a man. The flash on his collar became a tiepin. The silhouette of him fell on a floor of large linoleum squares. The pain came from my genitals. And his fur became hair on his chest and arms. And the smell of his breath . . . beer.

To this day, I can never sleep with a door cracked open even slightly at night. If a man has really hairy arms and he touches me, I would feel actual pain on my skin. I have refused to sleep with men with hairy chests. For a long time, if someone's breath smelled of beer, I would become instantly so angry at them I'd have to walk away. (Dating Bryant got me over that one!)

When I was in college, my best friend and I were taking Psychology 101 that you can imagine was an eye opener for me. We got to the chapter about hypnosis and regression therapy and if it's real or not. I decided I wanted to see if this could help my nightmares that at the age of 21 I was still having.

We went into one of the public bathrooms that no one really knew about as it was on the third floor of the fine arts performance center labeled "Powder Room". We would hide in there to study, talk or even nap.

We read the chapter and then she had me lay down on the French floral upholstery couch while she counted down and began to talk to me.

As they say, long story short, I ended up sitting upright screaming while she tried to wake me up. The door flew open and the cleaning lady looked terrified at my equally terrified expression.

We never attempted that again.

When I was 24, I read a book about dreams. In this book, the author explained that you could control your dreams if you want. Exhausted of having the same dream since a toddler, I decided to try it. I told myself before I fell asleep that I would open that door myself and find out what I needed to know. I would not wait until I couldn't move under the weight of whoever it was. I would find out who had raped me as a child.

I fell asleep and soon I was dreaming but this time I was an adult in bed and the door was built into a armoire. As the light began to shine behind it, I struggled with all my might to get out of bed to open the door and see who was on the other side. I made it out of the bed but as I reached for the door, it moved to the other side of the room and was now a glass door in a glass wall with frosted coating on it.

I turned to see myself laying in bed asleep. I began to pull at the door but it wouldn't open. The room began to get lighter and I could sense that daylight was coming and that I was running out of time. I felt my body being pulled back to the bed. I slipped back into my body. The room became dark again. The door became outlined with light. I screamed and felt pressure pushing me back into the bed. I screamed again and with all my might somehow the whole bed began moving towards the door. I let out an animal-like scream and growl. I felt the bed lurch. Then the bed with me in it slammed into the glass door and it shattered into pieces all around me. My arms and legs became free and I walked out of the room.

Say what you will but I have not had that nightmare since then. It was liberating not to have the dream anymore but I felt I had let myself down. I still didn't know who had done it to me. I couldn't stop them from doing it again to some other child. Was it someone at the bar who had put me to bed and helped himself? Was it someone who worked at the children's home? Was it one of the five foster homes I had been in? But of course, that answer never came and soon I felt guilty that I had liberated my soul perhaps at the expense of another child.

But I knew that I had survived and had begun recently thriving. Maybe it was time to let it all go and not let it in any way define me as a person and as a woman.

So, you can imagine my anger and my outrage at a higher power when at the age of 38 . . . it happened again.

I remember the music, salsa-style. I remember the man with the baby on the way cooking in my kitchen. I remember the man I had hung out with twice before laughing and dancing with me in my living room. I remember another man who said he was from Ohio just like me playing on my computer looking for Latin songs. I remember the girl whose brother was the one I was dancing with. And another man who had tried to kiss me at the club, and I had rejected.

Then I remember waking up to one of them inside of me, moving back and forth. I tried to move, speak but nothing happened.

I woke up again. Another one of them was now inside of me, grunting. This time I could feel a noise coming out of my throat. It started as a whimper and ended as a small scream.

"She's gonna start freaking out." I heard a voice say beside the bed. I found I could once again move and turned my head to see where the voice was coming from in my well-lit bedroom. I saw three of the men standing beside the bed and the one I had been dancing with had his phone in his hand holding it out in front of him. I could hear the clicking noise and I knew pictures were being taken. I tried to cry and scream and kick but my legs and feet felt heavy.

Suddenly, the boy from Ohio burst through the bedroom door

and pulled the man off of me. They fought. He won. He reached his arms towards me. Suddenly, my arms worked and I hit him.

"No, I've got you. No one is going to touch you." He began to scream at them to get out of the room as he struggled to get the covers over my naked body. Every time his fingers touched my skin it felt like hot irons being laid on my flesh. I flinched and writhed in a pain that left no physical mark.

He kept telling me over and over to be calm.

"We are both from Ohio, right? I'll take care of you. I'm sorry. I'm sorry. I've got you now. I've got you. No one's going to touch you."

That's the last thing I remember. I woke up the next morning with all my bed sheets laying on the floor and the bed frame six inches from the wall. I stumbled out into the kitchen to get some water. My head was throbbing and my throat was sore. The place was a mess with piles of dishes and food everywhere. I looked at the clock on the microwave and began to curse.

I had promised my friend Valerie that I would take her son to a car race for remote controlled cars. I couldn't stand him up. Valerie had tried to kill herself over a breakup two nights before and her son had been there. I had spent most of that night at her place patching her wrists and calming him down. He needed to go to this car race so that things were appearing in someway normal.

I got dressed quickly and didn't even take time to shower. My joints felt stiff and my head was not feeling any better.
As I began to walk to my car, I called my best friend Emily and told her about my night and what had happened. How odd it was that all of them were gone the next day.

I told her about waking up and having sex with the one that

had tried to kiss me. I thought I had a dream about one of them taking pictures.

"And they went through my phone and deleted all their numbers. Why would they do that?"

"What happened exactly?" Emily asked, her voice sounding tense.

I struggled to remember.

"I had been dancing then they poured me a drink and we ate some food. Then I woke up and I couldn't move. I passed out again and when I woke up I still couldn't move or make a noise. Then . . . this guy was on top of me . . . then another guy . . . I couldn't move . . . they were all taking pictures . . . Then the boy from Ohio got mad and told them that it was enough . . ."
I trailed off trying hard to make it all make sense.

"They deleted all their numbers. Why would they do that to my phone? Why . . ."

There was a long pause and then my friend in the smallest, least jarring way said. "Page, you were raped."

I fell to the ground. I heard her yell that she was on her way. I told her to stay with her kids or something like that not wanting even in this moment to put her out. I dialed my friend Jason who I had called my brother for over three years.

"Jason, I need your help."

"What's wrong?"

"I've been...I've been raped."

"Stay right there."

I lay outside my condo building on the sidewalk like a homeless woman because suddenly my legs wouldn't work, until his large, black truck pulled up. He picked me up and carried me into his truck, and then again inside the ER since it seemed that suddenly I no longer had enough strength to even breath. He went directly to the admitting nurse and whispered what had happened. They immediately began the usual protocol of how to handle a rape victim and rushed me through a side door into the back.

Soon Emily was there with a look that revealed neither pity nor fear, she was in what we call "mom-mode". I loved her so much for that.

She stood at the side of my bed as the doctor, a woman with red hair and freckles, started the rape kit. Holding my hand tightly, Emily just told me to look at her.

"I got you. I got you. We got this."

The rape counselor came in as the doctor was removing fifteen hairs from my head. Everything was moving so fast.

I instantly didn't like her and soon she proved why. In the middle of her "speech," she told me that it was my right not to press charges.

"But if you don't, they'll end up just doing it to someone else."

"I know," I said crying even harder.

"And you wouldn't want that on your conscience, right?"

"No," I gulped.

"Because if you don't follow through with the charges, they'll just get away with it and—"

"Hey!" Emily yelled from across the bed. "She gets it."

"Well, I was just trying to make sure that she knows—"

"Hey! You know what, you need to leave."

"But I—"

Emily let go of my hand and walked around the bed towards the counselor who now looked quite afraid even though Emily was half her height and weight. Like I said, "mom-mode."

"Give me your card and your pamphlets and get out."

My brother on an errand to get me some coffee ran into the woman in the hallway. She promptly informed him that my friend was rude. My brother apologized to her. As she got her papers back in order and they chatted, she stepped into it yet again.

"So I heard from the police that it was some Mexicans who did it. I tell you it's always either the blacks or the Hispanics. It's like a thing with them."

My brother looked at her like she had suddenly grown a second head and walked away.

As we moved onto the vaginal exam and the doctor was pulling 15 pubic hairs out (which by the way can I say is very painful!), the door suddenly flew open, the cloth curtain yanked back and a large man stood there.

"Hey, they said I could find a cop in here."

I don't know who lunged at the dumbass first who was busy staring at my vagina, the doctor or Emily, but I remember thinking what just happened and I hoped the doctor hadn't lost count and would have to start over.

Before Emily slammed the door shut, she leaned out to tell my brother to stand guard.

"God damn it. It's like raping her all over again. Shit." Emily said as came back to the side of the bed.

The three-ring circus continued when the two male cops arrived. By then, I had finished the pelvic swabbing, the shining of the blue light to see semen and the lovely speech while downing morning after pill, antibiotics, STD ward-off pills, and an AIDS test, that I would have to be tested in another six months for all possible diseases and not to have unprotected sex.

As the sedative kicked in and my crying and screaming had stopped, the rage inside kept growing. I could not fathom a God or a higher power that would expect a woman to survive this twice.

My whole life I had been taught that God was my heavenly father. My earthly father had pimped me out. Some other man raped me. And now the God of Love raped me. He sat in the corner with His arms crossed and did nothing while a little, white-haired girl was raped and then sat in the corner and watched while doing what? Reading a magazine? Doing a crossword? Picking lotto numbers?

Two weeks later with everyone gone to their families' Thanksgiving celebrations, I sat alone in my living room. Sure I had plenty of pity invitations, but I was still seriously depressed and pissed off.
I sat there with a beautiful bowl full of colorful candy in front of me.

Okay, it was a bowl full of pain medication, allergy medicine, muscle relaxers, sleeping pills, anything I could find in my roommate's bathroom, and even a few expired narcotics from a back injury four years earlier.

There they sat. All bright pink, striped blues, angry looking reds, hot oranges, ordinary whites, see-through blue-greens, and oddly calming pale yellows. I put them purposely in a white bowl. (Even if you are thinking of killing yourself, you should do it in an eye pleasing, Martha Stewart-way.)

I had shaved my legs, plucked my eyebrows and taken a shower. No reason for a medical examiner to see me not thoroughly groomed. I sat cross-legged on my couch facing a black tv screen thinking of recent events and how I had let it happen. I saw my reflection in the TV screen and remembered that thank god I had had the foresight to have those pictures taken so that the news story about my death would have good photos.

Hours went by as I sat in front of that colorful bowl of death candy, and I began to wonder what it would be like to just drink a bottle of great wine, down some random mixture of meds and go to sleep. Daydreaming about what would happen after I gently went into that good night. Who would care? Would some preacher stand over my grave and tell how much God loved me? Would my adopted mother come and shake her head like she knew all along I was unstable? There was even a moment of dreaming of God at the gates of Heaven telling me I couldn't come in because I had done this and me telling Him to kiss my ass and stop being so unimportant in the world and allowing people to get hurt while telling us He loves us.

You are probably wondering after all the horrid things that had been dumped into my life why I would now, of all times, be considering suicide.

I don't think I really was. It was a point I had to make to myself and to the Higher Power. He could pick me up at will since a child and use me as his favorite stress toy all he/she wanted. But this, this moment, I had the power. And I needed . . . no, I craved feeling powerful again.

No one defines you but you. No one tells you your path in life but you. Sure I could easily drink myself to death or do drugs. I of all people could justify it. Doctors would justify it as they wrote me prescription after prescription. Therapists would tell me it was understandable given my history. I could have people shake their heads and say they understood how it came to this. I could even pull off sympathy from the viewing audience if I ever made an episode of "Intervention."

But then, who wins?

No, I decide my worth and no one else. And I'll be damned straight to hell if I don't thrive in this lifetime.

So, I put away the pills and soon started on this book. After all, there is nothing saying that the photo you had picked out for your obit can't be used for the back cover of your memoir, right?

NINE

Person: My Biological Brother

Lesson: There is a difference between a "slut" and a "whore".

Lesson: Labels should be for clothes only.

So for almost four years, I was what you could only call a "whore." From age 24-29, I had been faithful to my husband. Then immediately followed Bryant for five years. A couple one night stands, then Darron for a few months, then David for three years - off and on. After the rape was worse since I seemed to want to find my power back by deciding whom I did and did not sleep with. So for about a total time period of about four years, I slept with 102 people. Mostly men, a few girls, a few threesomes.

The night I laid breathing heavy from the latest young Marine workout session (after all, I did my patriotic duty as much as possible!), I realized that I had indeed crossed over into the triple digits.

I didn't know if I should tell the guy. Like hand him one of those large checks, or maybe confetti should fall from the ceiling. Since it wasn't really good sex, I decided to let him be oblivious.

The next morning, I walked into Emily's office and flopped down dramatically into a chair.

"I've done it. It's official, I'm a whore."

Without even looking up from her paperwork, she contradicted me. Not to say that I was not a whore but to correct my grammar.

"I think a 'whore' gets paid for it, a 'slut' gives it away." She suddenly looked up at me. "Did you—?"

"No! God, I wish I could get paid for it. Some of them definitely should have paid me."

She went back to her work. I decided the confessional session couldn't end without me getting some kind of absolution.

"Ok, so I'm a slut."

"What brought this sudden revelation on?"

"Triple digits. I'm in the triple digits."

"Hmmmmm."

I stared at the top of her head.

"Hmmmm? That's what you have to say? By the way, you have GOT to dye your roots. Damn."

"What do you want me to say? And I know, I bought the dye yesterday."

"I don't know."

"You're not a slut. You just did what millions of men for centuries have done. No one calls them sluts. They get all high fives and 'dude'! You don't have a boyfriend or a husband or a girlfriend, or kids, or even for god's sake, a mortgage. So why not do what or who you want?"

"So, I shouldn't feel bad about it?"

"Do you?"

I thought about it for a moment.

"I feel bad that I don't feel bad. I mean, that should be a sure sign of sluttiness, right?"

"Would you do it any differently if you could?"

"I'd probably not fake so many orgasms."

"Well, there you go."

"But didn't I just become what my adopted mom knew all along I would be?"

She clicked off her computer screen and looked at me with one of her "Mom" looks.

"If you mean a loving, caring, almost too caring, independent woman who survived all her bullshit and fucks whoever she wants, and loves whoever she wants, then yes, she was right all along."

We sat and stared at each other, and because she loves me, she didn't make fun of the tears beginning to form in my eyes.

"Seriously, Em, color your gray head tonight."

"Yeah, well, maybe you want to paint in the other nine nails with color instead of looking like white trash."

That, readers, is a friend.

It got me thinking though. How many labels could be put on me? Sister, friend, abuse survivor, abandoned child, rape survivor, child rape survivor, screenwriter, wife, ex-wife, girlfriend, daughter, adopted, abandoned, lover, whore, Christian, atheist, budding Buddhist, world traveller, granddaughter, cousin, niece, writer, domestic violence survivor….

The one that kept sticking in my head was "sister".

My first attempt at it had been a colossal failure. My adopted brother and I never really got along. Maybe it was because his mother so obviously thought he walked on water. Also it might be that she told me the following nuggets of truth:

"I never wanted another child."

"I never wanted a daughter, little girls are all so evil and conniving."

"I asked him if he wanted a little brother or little sister. He insisted a sister and I couldn't talk him out of it."

"I read an article in the doctor's office that said that only children suffer socially. So I basically bought you as a playmate for him."

Somehow, this did not endure him or her to me.

However, I knew from my conversation with my biological mom that I had a half-brother. It had now been several years since I'd had that first talk with her, which meant he was safely out of high school, so I couldn't think that I would ruin his life with the news of my existence.

I had googled him over the years but never found anything. In my 39th year, I decided to search on the now famous Facebook. I typed in his name and his profile popped up. Just like that . . . internet magic!

I sat there for hours not knowing what to say. What do you say? And knowing that once I sent it, I couldn't take it back and his life, his family's life and our mother's life would never be the same.

Familiar fear of rejection choked me and my fingers hovered over the keys until they began to cramp. I didn't even notice that it had gotten dark outside and only the light in the room was from the keyboard.

There were two sides to this conundrum. I had let our mother control both of our lives. Let her reject me and walk away once again. Thoughts of anger and grief and pain filled my head until it hurt. On the other hand, he was innocent in all this and he would never look at her the same. He would be forced to either reject me and keep her or keep her and reject me. I knew somehow in my heart that these would be her terms.

One thing about this decade that I have learned is that sometimes you have to do what is right for you. It's okay to be selfish sometimes. But could I be THAT selfish?

I stayed up all night writing draft after draft of an email to send to him. I went ahead and friend requested him to test and see if he would accept. Maybe he knew about me already. By morning, he had accepted my friend request. I saw the email icon tell me I had one in my inbox. I clicked on it and there was an email for me.

> Zach
> Thanks for the friend request. I'm curious. How do we know each other?

Talk about a loaded question. Well, it was now or never. Carefully, I typed in my response.

> Page
> I'm not sure. Are you the son of Shirley ———- of Marion, Ohio? And do you have an Aunt Jess?

> Zach
> Yes, I do . . . now you have me really curious.

> Page
> I know this is going to be hard to believe

but I'm your big sister. I was born in 1969 to your mom before she met your father. I think she should explain to you. Not me. I don't want to cause problems. Just thought you had the right to know. Hope to hear from you soon.

Zach

that's an interesting story now who are you really? and why exactly did you pick me to try and cause drama?

Well, this isn't going well so far, I thought. Maybe I'd made a mistake.

Page

I'm not. I just thought you had a right to now that I exist. I meant no harm. Forgive me. I won't contact you again.

Zach

you can contact me if you want i just find your story to be ridiculous, but maybe its not....who is our father?   how did he know my mom? why have i not heard anything about this before?

Page

I talked to both your mom (mine too) and Aunt Janet, I think you need to talk to them first because I'm sure you won't believe anything I say since you don't know me. Ask your mom. I was born Martha Pauley to our mom and Robert Pauley was my dad. My name was changed when I was adopted.

Zach

when did you talk to my mom?

Page

Your senior year of high school. Seriously, I feel terrible about disrupting your world. Your mom did what she needed to do for herself I understand. I have no family and wanted to reach out. Please forgive me for any drama.

Zach

Your not really disrupting anything. I haven't talked to hear about this, I don't know if I will or not and I have no relationship with Aunt Janet at all so I'm not asking her for any kind of conformation of you and this story.
But why now?!?! If you've known you're my sister then why wait so long to say anything?

I had to drive into work at this point. By the time I got there about 15 minutes later, Facebook let me know I had a new message.

Zach

Wow so I talked to my mom and she said it's true.

I couldn't believe it! She actually admitted it! To the child she had chosen to love, to shelter, to keep free of the knowledge of her huge secret! I can't really tell you what that felt like. If you could smush the words: excited, nauseous, elated, saddened, dizzy, vindicated, and relieved into one magnificent word . . . well, that would be the word for it.

> Zach
>
> I don't know what to say! don't know what to say, damn I wrote that twice and didn't even notice. I thought this kinda shit only happened in lifetime movies. This is very surreal. i don't know what to do. i never even suspected I had a sister. do you have kids? are you married? are you happy? who are you? what do you like? what are you like?

I chuckled to myself. Good questions. That's what I'd been working on answering these last few years.

> Zach
>
> I wish I would have known. if you called her when i was in high school why the hell didn't i know about it? why do you get to know about e and i don't get to know about you until now? I'm not mad. i just wish i would have known.

And now, let's put that bus in reverse and run over her.

> Page
>
> Our mom asked me to never say anything to you as she was sure you would hate her. I didn't want to upset

you your senior year of high school and then…I just figured you deserved a drama-free life unlike the one I've had. But I've always thought of you. I have pics of you that Aunt Jess sent. Maybe we could set up a time to talk on the phone soon.

Zach

I wouldn't have hated her. I hated finding out like this and I would have liked to have known senior year.
School was never a big deal to me anyway. I'm glad you thought of me. I always wanted a bro or a sis. I wonder what's worse? Thinking about what a sibling is doing that you don't even know or wondering what it would be like to have a sibling to begin with. I never had the option of knowing about you. That hurts more then anything. I understand why she gave you up. I don't know how much you know about your birth fa ther but my (I mean "our" mom - weird) didn't speak too highly of him. And don't get me wrong, I'm glad you contacted me and I'm glad i know of you now. I can bitch and moan till I'm blue in the face but it won't change anything about the how's and why's of why i was never told. i kinda feel like my whole childhood was fake. my dad never said anything either—damn.

Page

Your dad didn't know until the day I first called our mom. She never told him. He was pretty upset.

> Zach
>
> My wife had a similar thing happen to her, i mean, the other way around. She had a kid before me, a daughter. She gave her up for adoption too. Difference is that my kids and I know about it. She didn't hide it from me. i wanna know you and i wanna know about you. Tell me about what drama you've dealt with. tell me about you. I'm gonna have to work up to the phone call but i would like to talk to you eventually. This is just alot to take in all at once.

I told him all I knew about our mom and my dad. About my adopted home, foster homes. That I played piano. Went to college. I'm a writer and graphic designer. He said he never went to college, couldn't draw a straight line and didn't play any instruments. I said I had no kids and wasn't married. He said he had two children both with disabilities and was married. I explained the bad situation with my adopted mom. Then, he said.

> Zach
>
> I had a decent childhood. Never had a lot of money but mom and dad were good to me. She lives next door in the apartment beside us.

Had I just read that right? She lived next door! I felt my head start to feel like my brain was on a tilt-a-whirl while my body was lock-kneed around it. I plopped down quickly into my office chair before I hit the floor. I collected myself. Was it time to once again put myself out there? Sit back down on that floor beside my dog and wait for her to choose? I put my hands up to the keyboard then back into my lap about a dozen times before I told myself to suck it up and do it. I noticed that my fingertips were tingly as I slowly typed back.

> Page
> Let her know that she can mail me a letter or call me or email me if she wants, you know, to know about me.
>
> Zach
> Mom email? LOL. She can't use a computer. But I'll tell her what you said.

I waited for what seemed to be an eternity. I could envision him running back over to our mom's apartment and telling her what I had typed. Would she jump up and eagerly ask him to type in something from her? I actually smiled at the absurdity of that. Did she look at him with that same look she gave me and my dog? Trying to decide who to keep - my brother or me?

A couple hours went by and I thought I now know what it felt like to live through the entire Dark Ages. Then my computer beeped that I had a message. I slowly opened my account. It felt like one of those bomb squad robots that ever so slowly lifts the edge of a package to see the contents all the while not sure if it would suddenly blow up.

> Zach
> She said that she doesn't want to talk to you. It's just too much for her.

I heard in the distance the sound of a door slamming shut once again and the faint sound of a dog's leash clanging against its collar.

Too much for her? What else did she have to lose? Her son knew now. The proverbial cat was out running wild now out of its bag. I ripped my computer out of its charger cord and ran into Emily's office, slamming it onto her desk and wordlessly pointing at the screen.

Loving her for yet another great quality, that she could read fast, I waited with tears running down my face.

"I'm sorry, babe. That really sucks." She gave me a hug and let me cry.

"Maybe it's for the best. I doubt he had such a great childhood. He's probably just saying that. I mean, she couldn't have been that great. And do you really want her drama in your life? She's just not a good person."

I looked up with mascara stains under my eyes and whispered.

"I just wish this time, just one time, she'd let me make the choice."

For a few weeks, my brother and I emailed almost every day. Finding out what likes and dislikes we had. Thanksgiving came and went and for the first time in a long time that family holiday bothered me. I was well into a bottle of shiraz on an empty stomach when I began picturing my brother's family walking next door to our mom's apartment for a turkey dinner. They all took their places around the table and began to eat. Was there an empty chair at the table? Did anyone look at it and think of me? Was I mentioned at all? Did my brother hold out until the pies were cut to blurt out "how could you?" to our mother? Did he study her face while she sipped her after dinner coffee?

So it had come full circle. Here I was at this place in my journey in finding myself and I knew the same thing as when I started . . . I would never have a mother. I would need to find my nurturing from friends. I would need to learn to love myself and give myself all the things I never got from a mother. And really, wasn't what this whole thing had at its core been about?

Finding out the woman I was, the woman I wanted to be, and the woman I never wanted to be . . . my biological mother.

EPILOGUE

There were three things I was scared of at a young age besides my new mother. One had to do with false teeth, the next snakes, and the last old-timey family photos.

When I was first adopted, there were still alive a few great-uncles. One was Great Uncle Cecil who lived in my grandparents upstairs spare room. The other was Great Uncle Orville. These were my grandfather's brothers.

In my grandfather's house, when you walked from the kitchen into the living room, my grandpa sat in his large recliner on the right, and Great Uncle Cecil on the couch on the left making a rather narrow entryway.

I had passed by them into the kitchen through their horrendous snoring where they would literally take turns. In the kitchen, I grabbed a glass of iced tea and went to return to the living room.

As I rounded the corner with glass in hand, suddenly something didn't seem right. I noticed too late that the snoring had stopped. I looked up to see an old hand holding a pair of stained dentures at my eye-level. The teeth snapped shut. Then, on my swirl to get away from them, another pair appeared at my other side. They both began to chatter just like the plastic teeth that you wind up.

I dropped the glass and went screaming to Grams in the kitchen. "Graaaaaaaams! Graaaaaaaaams!"

It took a while for me to calm down. During that time, Grams waddled into the living room and gave them a "what for" for scaring me half to death. There was something about the Page men that you couldn't stay mad at. They all had warm eyes that brightly twinkled with mischief and life.

After a few more times of this prank, I took to looking around the corner before entering the living room when they were both at their "battle stations".

As for making me scared of snakes . . . that honor goes to my adopted dad. When I was about 7, I found a garter snake in our garage. I yelled for Dad to come look. He came in, and carefully picked up the slender, foot long creature.

I bent over to look at it carefully, and that is the time that my father decided to thrust it into my face and instruct me that it could and probably would bite me. I took off running, screaming with him chasing me as best he could in his worker's steel-toed boots. Down a small hill, around the vegetable garden and back towards the garage, I ran as fast as I could.

He grew tired of running or of his game and with great aim from his high school football days, threw the snake onto the back of my neck where it wiggled down the inside of my shirt.

I almost blacked out from terror. He laughed so long that I thought he'd black out from lack of oxygen.

Fear is a funny thing. When I turned 32, I started to make a list of my top three fears and my top three goals. If by the time my next birthday rolled around and I hadn't done them all, then I did not consider myself a success that year. It was a kind of New Years Resolution List but on October 13th.

My list last year for the ripe age of 40 contained for fears: 1) Holding a snake, 2) Writing a complete book (this is it!), 3) Living alone.

I had done pretty much #2 and #3 but it was a week away from my birthday and I still had #1 to do. As usual, the Universe will give you what you ask for.

I was walking down the sidewalk in the small Southern town I had made my home for the last ten years and there in the middle of the sidewalk was a rather large black man with dreads holding an even bigger snake. It was wrapped around his neck and flicking its tongue.

The usual fear filled my throat. I didn't even want to walk by it. I started to cross the street but—I mean, it was a snake and my birthday was almost upon me.

I turned and walked up to the gentleman.

"Hi, I know this is going to sound strange but I do this thing where I have to face at least three of my fears every year. I'm down to the last one and it's holding a snake. I just wondered if maybe I could hold yours?"

The man looked at me and I figured he would either say, "fuck off" or "you're crazy" or "you need therapy". Instead, he smiled and slowly lifted the snake off of his shoulders and began to place it onto mine.

"Now, be careful. She's gentle but she can sense fear."

It's a good thing that the snake was already on my shoulders when he decided to say that otherwise I would have flinched and run screaming.

I knew I had to immediately calm my pounding heart and even out my breathing. The snake was cool to the touch, heavy and graceful. She let me hold her head as she lightly flicked my skin with her tongue.

"Hey, everyone, this young lady is terrified of snakes. She's facing her fear. How about that?"

Suddenly, people were taking pics of me and clapping at my success. I really wanted them to stop clapping as I'm sure that would not make Ms. Snake very happy but it still was kinda nice.

Someone took a pic of me on my iphone. You can see the pride, the fear, and the joy in my eyes.

It's like whatever you have to do to conquer a fear is never as bad as the fear itself.

That's what I've learned about this journey so far.

So, for my 40's, my fears to overcome are these.
1) Learn to salsa and do it in public (preferably with a hot Latin).
2) Print this book and do a live reading
3) Learn to fully love the me I have become because of my 30's.
4) Embrace that inner little girl and love her like a mother should have loved her.

Lost: Woman, Found: Child

ABOUT THE AUTHOR

M. Page Jones wrote her first story in first grade and has never stopped. Holding a B.A. in Creative Writing, Jones spent years as a screenwriter, film producer, and graphic artist. She is a published author with screenplays, short stories and textbooks. This is her first memoir, but the next one about life in her 40's has already begun.

www.ingramcontent.com/pod-product-compliance
Lightning Source LLC
Chambersburg PA
CBHW060835050426
42453CB00008B/702